UNIVERSITY ASSOCIATES
Publishers and Consultants

SERIES IN HUMAN RELATIONS TRAINING

Reference Guide to Handbooks and Annuals

J. William Pfeiffer, Ph.D.
Human Relations Consultant
La Jolla, California

John E. Jones, Ph.D.
Human Relations Consultant
La Jolla, California

UNIVERSITY ASSOCIATES
Publishers and Consultants
7596 Eads Avenue
La Jolla, California 92037

PREFACE

The nine books whose contents are classified in this edition of the *Reference Guide* contain a large number of useful materials—structured experiences, instruments, lecturettes, theory and practice papers, book reviews, and resources. Access to these tools, techniques, and ideas is made difficult by the serial nature of their publication. Occasionally even we, the editors, find it frustrating not to be able to locate a particular structured experience or paper in a hurry.

The first version of the *Reference Guide* was received so enthusiastically by users of the Pfeiffer and Jones Series in Human Relations Training that we decided to improve its usefulness and expand its coverage. This new edition includes classifications of *all* the contents of nine books: the five volumes of *A Handbook of Structured Experiences for Human Relations Training* and the four volumes of *The Annual Handbook for Group Facilitators.*

In addition to categorizing contents, we have drawn together much of the material that we have written about the rapidly expanding developments in the human relations field. In the introductions to the sections of the *Annuals* we have treated a number of topics related to the use of structured experiences, instruments, and lecturettes. We have also commented on the shape and progress of theory and research. These useful background materials have been collected and integrated into this edition of the *Reference Guide.*

We intend to update this publication periodically, to incorporate new material that we have issued. Suggestions for improvement in format, content, etc., are welcomed.

We are also interested in continuing to receive manuscripts for possible inclusion in the Pfeiffer and Jones Series in Human Relations Training. Users may submit structured experiences, instruments, lecturettes, theory and practice papers, and comments on resources available to the practicing group facilitator and organization development consultant. We have developed an informational pamphlet to guide contributors in preparing manuscripts for our review; copies are available on request.

The original idea for a reference guide was developed by René Robitaille, who was enrolled in the first year of our Laboratory Education Intern Program. We are grateful for his contribution.

The *Handbooks* and the *Annuals* are now appearing in several foreign languages. We feel very pleased to be instrumental in making these materials widely available to persons interested in improving the private and working lives of people. We also are gratified that the number of people who use our materials continues to grow every year. Our publishing aim is to share the useful and valuable information that we collect in the human relations training field. It is in this spirit that the *Reference Guide to Handbooks and Annuals* has been prepared.

J. William Pfeiffer
John E. Jones

La Jolla, California
June, 1975

TABLE OF CONTENTS

INTRODUCTION

The *Reference Guide to Handbooks and Annuals* is intended for use by group facilitators, organization development (OD) consultants, students, and others interested in applied behavioral science. Because the book contains discussions of many facets of experience-based learning, it can be used as an ancillary text as well as a reference source.

Classifications of each of the types of material included in *A Handbook of Structured Experiences for Human Relations Training* and *The Annual Handbook for Group Facilitators* are preceded by introductory statements that provide background or related information. These materials have been taken from the introductions to the five sections of the *Annuals*. We have also included in its entirety our paper on design from the 1973 *Annual*.

In each section—structured experiences, instruments, lecturettes, theory and practice papers, and resources—the titles are first organized into appropriate categories according to subject area and then, within each category, listed in order of their publication date.

Following the classification of all five sections is a listing that indicates how the categories treated in this *Reference Guide* are related to each other and shows in what section or sections each category is used. At the end of the guide is both a name and a title index.

This guide can be used in several ways. It can be studied for its collected information on the technology of human relations training. Facilitators can use it for design ideas for laboratories, workshops, conferences, meetings, seminars, institutes, and OD interventions. A particular piece published in the nine-book *Handbook* and *Annual* series can be located either by title or by author. Materials related to each other in subject matter, such as structured experiences and instruments in OD, can be cross-referenced.

CLASSIFICATION OF DESIGN COMPONENTS

The following chart* illustrates the relationship between learner involvement and the locus of meaning in human relations training. With *experiential* approaches—those that primarily stress active participant involvement vs. passive receptivity—the learning is presumably internalized more effectively.

---

*Based in part on Hall's learning involvement continuum and Tannenbaum and Schmidt's continuum of leadership behavior.

THE TECHNOLOGY OF HUMAN RELATIONS TRAINING

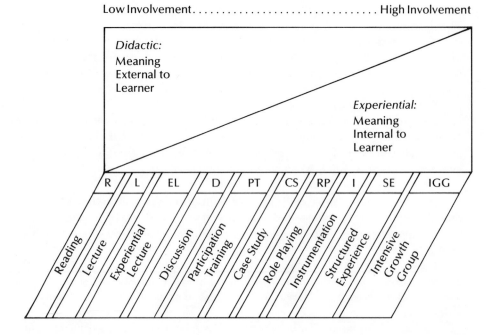

Low Involvement. . . . . High Involvement

Reading along the bottom of the chart, we see a classification of human relations training design components, ordered according to the extent to which they incorporate learner involvement. The least involving intervention is reading, in which the learner is in a *reactive* mode, passively receiving and vicariously experiencing. The most involving intervention is the intensive growth group, in which the learner is encouraged to be *proactive,* to take responsibility for his own learning. In between these two extremes are activities that range from lectures to structured experiences.

The experiential lecture is more involving than the traditional lecture approach because it incorporates activities on the part of the "audience." Interspersed among the sections of content are brief interactions among participants. These interruptions are designed either to personalize the points of the lecture and/or to generate readiness for the next topic.

Discussion is a time-honored teaching intervention, which has been extended and refined in participation training, particularly by adult educators at Indiana University. The case-study method, popular in business education, is closely related to role playing, in which a "case" is acted out in a semistructured format.

In instrumentation, which involves learners in self-assessment, the didactic component comes from the theory underlying the items of the scale. Structured experiences stress high participation and "processing" of data generated during interactive activities.

Intensive growth groups exist in many forms, such as counseling, T-groups, encounter, and therapy. They are characterized by high learner involvement and interaction. The data for learning come from the life experiences and here-and-now reactions of the group members. Participants are expected to integrate their learning into new self-concepts on their own terms.

The involvement continuum in the chart can be seen in the same relationship to other dimensions, such as risk, self-disclosure, and interaction. Each design component is useful for a different purpose, and there are training situations in which each would be appropriate.

Facilitators are continually faced with the task of planning activities to meet the learning needs of participants. The design problem can be graphically represented as follows:

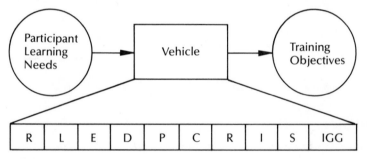

The choice of an effective intervention is made after an assessment of the learning needs of participants and a statement of training objectives. The maturity of the group, the skill and experience of the facilitator, and the environment in which the training takes place determine which approach is used.

AN EXPERIENTIAL MODEL

Structured experiences are designed to implement an experiential model, which is based on a cyclical learning process of five separate but interlocking procedures. As implied by the name of the model, the emphasis is on the *direct* experiences of the participant or learner—as opposed to the *vicarious* experiences garnered through didactic approaches.

The experiential model is also an *inductive* rather than a *deductive* process: the participant *discovers* for himself the learnings offered by the experiential process. His discovery may be facilitated by a leader, but in the end the participant finds and validates his own experience.

This is the "laboratory"—or experimental—approach to learning. It is based on the premise that experience precedes learning and that the learning, or meaning, to be derived from any experience comes from the learner himself. Any individual's experience is unique to himself; no one can tell him what he is to learn, or gain, from any activity. Probable learnings can, of course, be devised, but it is up to the participant to validate these for himself.

Five revolving steps are included in the experiential model.

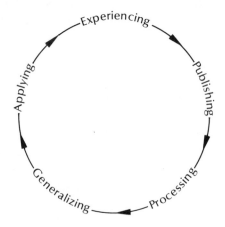

Experiencing

The process usually starts with experiencing. The participant becomes involved in an activity; he *acts* or *behaves* in some way or he *does, performs, observes, sees, says* something. This initial experience is the basis for the entire process.

Publishing

Following the experience itself, it becomes important for the participant to share or "publish" his reactions and observations with others who have either experienced or observed the same activity.

Processing

Sharing one's reactions is only the first step. An essential—and often neglected—part of the cycle is the necessary integration of this sharing. The dynamics that emerged in the activity are explored, discussed, and evaluated (processed) with other participants.

Generalizing

Flowing logically from the processing step is the need to develop principles or extract generalizations from the experience. Stating learnings in this way can help participants further define, clarify, and elaborate them.

Applying

The final step in the cycle is to plan applications of the principles derived from the experience. The experiential process is not complete until a new learning or discovery is used and tested behaviorally. This is the "experimental" part of the experiential model. Applying, of course, becomes an experience in itself, and, with new experience, the cycle begins again.

NOTES ON TERMINOLOGY

Human relations trainers are notorious for their use of jargon. Facilitators using an "applied-behavioral-science" approach often use technical terms interchangeably, adding to the confusion of participants. The following listing is intended to help clarify this situation.

Structured Experience	A design that implements an experiential model (experiencing, publishing, processing, generalizing, applying) by focusing on particular learning goals.
Exercise	The practice, repetition, or solidification of new behavior; skill building. May follow a structured experience.
Experiment	A structured activity with unpredictable outcomes.
Game	Connotes fun; emphasis is on the activity itself; often is not serious in intent; may incorporate competition, deception, and chance.
Simulation	A microcosmic activity reflecting a larger universe; implies the simplification of complex phenomena, a cognitive emphasis, and the use of external reality. Oriented toward process rather than toward personal integration.
Package	A self-contained series of activities, instruments, designs, and/or audio-visual aids; frequently self-directing.

Although these terms are not technically precise, we have found it useful to insist on making sharp distinctions between them for the sake of clarity and ease of comprehension. Undoubtedly many persons would argue for even more specific and exclusive definitions. We invented the term "structured experience," for example, to emphasize the two aspects of that intervention: the existence of some boundaries and the process of learning through doing.

DESIGN CONSIDERATIONS IN LABORATORY EDUCATION*

J. William Pfeiffer and John E. Jones
(Originally published in *The 1973 Annual Handbook for Group Facilitators*)

One of the most complex activities in which the group facilitator/human relations consultant is engaged is designing learning experiences for client systems. The purpose of this paper is to discuss some of the determinants of effectiveness in laboratory-education design in general and to explore the major considerations that the facilitator needs to relate to as he designs laboratories focusing on personal growth and leadership development.

Whether one is planning a course in human relations, a weekend personal growth laboratory, or a management development seminar, there are common concerns and questions that need to be considered in order for an optimum design to emerge. We will begin by cataloguing the major parameters that need to be specified before designs can be built, the skills involved in designing laboratory-education events, components of the laboratory itself, and considerations that must be taken into account in meeting the unique needs of the client system. The primary emphasis will be on integrating these general design considerations into an organic sequencing of learning activities that we have found to be central to personal growth and leadership development laboratories. In addition, we have included suggestions concerning professional development in the area of design.

MAJOR DESIGN PARAMETERS

Before the design itself can be considered, there are several questions that must be answered concerning the specific learning experience being planned. The purpose of this section is to provide an explicit check list of these concerns which the facilitator

---

*Laboratory education has been operationally defined by the International Association of Applied Social Scientists as events that include T-groups (semistructured) and D-groups (structured). This definition *excludes* personal growth groups ("structureless"), which the organization defines in terms of psychotherapy—groups that have an emergent design rather than a previously planned design. However, the authors have some concern that the term "T-group" has come to incorporate a variety of meanings to professionals and to lay people, including some negative connotations; therefore, we prefer to use the term "personal growth" as having the semistructured dimensions that IAASS defines as T-group experiences.

may use in testing his own readiness to begin the design process. He is ready to design when he has data about the following:

1. the contract
2. the length and timing of the event
3. the location and physical facilities
4. the familiarity of participants with each other
5. the training experience of the participants
6. the availability of qualified staff
7. the number of participants
8. access to materials and other aids
9. the opportunity for follow-through.

Contract. Although the previous list is not rank-ordered in terms of urgency, the first item is perhaps the most important. It is critical that the facilitator have a clear sense of what the contract between himself and the client system is. This consideration relates to his skill in specifying goals. It is important that he be able to narrow the expectation gap between himself and the participants in the laboratory. It is also important that he recognize that the psychological contract and the legal contract may not be one and the same. The design is far more likely to have a chance to be effective if the participants come into the learning experience knowing what to expect, why they are there, and what they have contracted to experience. The facilitator may choose to negotiate such a contract explicitly with the client system (e.g., Egan's model contract, contained in the 1972 *Annual*) or the facilitator may choose simply to rely on a word-of-mouth or a brochure procedure to specify the learning goals of the event. In any case, it is important that the goals and the learning method of the event be specifiable beforehand in language that both staff and participants can understand.

Length and Timing of the Event. The length and timing of the laboratory are important in that the sequencing and timing of particular events are dependent in part on whether the laboratory takes place en masse or is spaced over several meetings. The laboratory that runs weekly for an hour or two presents a significantly different design problem than a weekend event. In a brief contact design, such as one evening or one or two days, some learning modules would not be attempted because either there would not be enough trust developed in the time available or more data might be generated than could be adequately processed in the time allowed.

Location and Physical Facilities. The third parameter is important in that it is easier to develop what is called a "cultural-island" effect in a retreat setting than it is in the ordinary, everyday environment of the participants. It is more possible in a retreat situation to capitalize on the development of norms of meaningful openness, experimentation, and sensitivity in creating an environment in which people are genuinely resourceful to each other during the free time of the laboratory event. It is often noted that some of the most significant learning in human relations training takes place outside these formally planned sessions. The physical facilities are critical; ordinarily the facilitator wants to have movable furniture and privacy for the training event. Auditoriums are usually too inflexible for training sites, and sometimes very large open spaces can work to the detriment of the laboratory design. It is important to anticipate whether the training event is likely to be interrupted by nonparticipants, telephone calls, and other annoyances.

Familiarity of Participants with Each Other. This parameter is important in laboratory design in terms of selecting learning experiences. It may not be necessary to include "ice-breaker" training activities with a group of people who are familiar with each other. What often happens is that some participants know each other, but there is an unequal acquaintanceship within the group. The design of the laboratory should take into account that there might be some natural subdivision owing to previous social acquaintance outside the laboratory itself. It may be desirable to use this information in forming groups, assigning staff to the particular groups, and selecting activities for the beginning and the end of the experience. One may capitalize on the relationships that participants bring to a laboratory experience by using acquaintanceship as a means of support for planning back-home application and for follow-through.

Training Experience of Participants. Whether participants have been in laboratory-education programs before is important because they may already have experienced some kinds of training activities in which learning depends on the novelty of the experience to the participants. It may be that the clients will have been engaged in activities highly similar to those that are being planned, and it makes most sense to know something of the background of participants in regard to experiential approaches to education before the design is attempted. People who have been in laboratory experiences before may be formed into an advanced group, they may be spread out deliberately across several learning groups, or they may be asked to volunteer for demonstrations of here-and-now interaction.

Availability of Qualified Staff. The sixth parameter is the availability of qualified staff to work as facilitators in the training program. The design of the experience should take into account the capabilities of the staff as well as their preparedness in attempting various learning goals. If the staff members are minimally qualified, it may be necessary to use a great deal of instrumentation and structure to make up for their lack of supervised experience. The intensity level of a laboratory may be modified and controlled somewhat depending on the expertise of the staff that is being assembled. Where the credentials of the staff are somewhat suspect, it may be necessary to develop fairly strict controls on the amount of affect that is generated in the laboratory experience itself. Activities that might be anticipated to generate a great deal of feeling data might be kept out of the design because in general they require a great deal more preparedness on the part of the staff.

Number of Participants. It is important to be able to anticipate how many people are likely to be involved in the laboratory setting because some laboratory design components require a large number of people while others are designed to be used in very small groups. In general, we recommend that there be co-facilitators in every intensive small group and that there be a pair of facilitators for about every ten to twelve participants.

Access to Materials and Other Aids. Availability, budget, and convenience are important considerations prior to planning a laboratory. Some materials, such as standardized measurement instruments, are expensive, and others require a great deal of preparation time for their assembly. Some teaching aids such as video-tape recorders are difficult to carry from place to place. The facilitator needs to develop an inventory of materials that are available both on-site and within his own resources: flip charts, chalkboards, overhead projectors and other audio-visual aids, as well as worksheets, instruments, and handouts. It is often very useful to have duplicating equipment at the laboratory setting.

Opportunity for Follow-Through. A final consideration deals with the opportunity to follow through with the laboratory participants after the experience is formally ended. Although this parameter is listed last, it is by no means of least importance. When developing a design for a learning event it is important to know beforehand what is going to happen afterwards. Is it going to be feasible for participants to meet again to work through the problems of transfer of training? Are they going to have access to each other on a day-to-day basis? Is the staff of the laboratory going to be accessible to them afterwards? Is it possible to have follow-up sessions some weeks or months later to ensure transfer of training? Part of the application of laboratory learning to one's own work and social setting can be designed differently if there is an opportunity for some support and follow-through work after the laboratory is completed.

Prior to developing the design for a particular training event, the facilitator needs to explore what he has to work with in terms of time, space, staff, money, human resources, and materials. Once he has completed such an inventory he may even conclude that the contracted goals of the learning experience are unattainable given the resources that are available to him, and he may want to renegotiate the contract or attempt to develop new resources for the event.

DESIGN SKILLS

Goal Setting. The ability to develop a learning design that is relevant and effective is dependent upon a number of skills on the part of the small-group facilitator. The major set of skills relates to the ability to identify the learning goals of the training event very specifically. It cannot be stressed enough that laboratory education is goal oriented, and it is important for the facilitator to learn ways to be able to clarify his goals for a particular training event or a particular part of a training event, so that these are motivators for the particular learning experience itself. A closely related set of skills involves helping participants clarify their own goals. It is important that human relations training activities be carried out in the light of highly specific goals that are related to the behavior of participants. In designing a laboratory, then, one begins with establishing, in a highly specific way, the goals of the experience.

Sensitivity to Participant Response. A second set of skills in designing laboratory-education events is sensitivity to participant response. The facilitator learns to anticipate how participants are likely to react to particular components of the laboratory design. In addition, he becomes adept at anticipating the cumulative effects of the design. He should be able to make some kinds of probability statements about the receptivity of participants to particular learning experiences at a particular point of the laboratory. Part of this sensitivity involves acquaintanceship with the client system. It is important that the facilitator be able to know how participants are likely to react to particular structured experiences and to particular foci within the laboratory. For example, if the laboratory is to begin with some kind of nonverbal exercise, how much tension is this likely to create in this particular client system at this particular point in its development? How are the same participants likely to react to a similar kind of activity after they have been together in a retreat setting for two days? Developing sensitivity to the probable participant response comes from experience with a variety of learning activities, with a variety of clients, and with a great deal of staff discussion of experiences in similar learning situations.

Sequencing. Sequencing constitutes a third set of skills in designing laboratories. Learning events are not put together in a random way; it is important that the facilitator be able to see the impact of one particular training component on the one that immediately follows it. Sometimes the objective is to close things down, but at other times the objective may be to open things up in order for the next training module to be more effective. One of the major purposes of this paper is to expand the group facilitator's awareness of sequencing considerations in personal growth and leadership development designs.

Collaborating with Other Facilitators. A fourth array of skills involves collaborating with other facilitators. In our experience it is more effective and efficient for one facilitator to accept responsibility for the initial design of the laboratory-education event and to work with other facilitators to edit the design to make it more relevant to the learning needs of the participants in light of the goals of the training event. It is expensive to bring together a group of facilitators to build a design from ground zero. It is true that when staff members create a design themselves, from the beginning, they are more likely to have a sense of investment, involvement, and psychological ownership in what is planned. They are likely to approach the implementation of the design with more vigor. It is also true, however, that human relations training staffs ordinarily do not have a great deal of time to prepare for a particular event. We find it useful to have an initial, tentative design that the staff will edit rather than build from the beginning. One of the major problems in designing laboratories centers around this set of skills. Many group facilitators have their own favorite ways of doing things and are sometimes reluctant to collaborate in experimenting with other teaching procedures. It is sadly ironic that often we get locked into particular ways of working in human relations training, and we violate our own norms of experimentation and innovation.

Modifying Designs. A fifth set of skills involves modifying designs while the laboratory is in progress. There is no way that any group facilitator can anticipate all the responses of participants and all the real-time concerns that become relevant in producing a plan of activities for fostering client learning. The facilitator needs to develop the ability to change the learning design while the laboratory is running. This involves taking data from participants about their own needs at a particular stage of the laboratory's development and finding appropriate alternatives to what was planned prior to the laboratory. When he discovers that what was planned back in the staff meeting before the laboratory began no longer makes sense in terms of what is happening now, he needs to be able to redirect the learning experience without becoming threatened by his lack of anticipation of participant response.

Skill in designing laboratory events involves learning how to make one's goals highly explicit and specific, learning to anticipate how particular participants are likely to respond to the various learning activities, learning to put laboratory components together in meaningful ways, developing the ability to collaborate with other facilitators in producing designs noncompetitively, and developing the ability to redirect the learning experience while it is in progress.

LABORATORY COMPONENTS

Designing human relations laboratories and leadership development laboratories involves putting together sequences of learning experiences in relation to the goals of the event. Four major components are ordinarily utilized. Some combination of intensive small groups, structured experiences, lecturettes, and instruments is employed to develop a community of learners who can collaborate in achieving the goals of the laboratory. The purpose of this section is to discuss each of these four components as integral parts of laboratory design.

Intensive Small Groups. There is an almost endless variety of small groups that have been developed within human interaction laboratories. The most common is the T-group, or training group, which is described in an earlier paper on types of growth groups (Jones, 1972). Other small-group designs incorporated into personal growth and leadership development laboratories include the D-group, or developmental group (Blake & Mouton, 1962). This is a group that uses a variety of questionnaires, rating scales, and other instruments and learning devices in the place of a trained facilitator. Sometimes laboratories include a variety of temporary groups that are put together on a short-term basis for processing the data of a particular learning exercise. Sometimes these groups are called N-groups, or new groups, assembled for the purpose of providing the opportunity for risk taking, trying of new behavior, or testing of back-home application ideas. In addition, it is sometimes desirable to build leaderless activities into laboratory events.

The dominant feature of laboratory education is the use of intensive small groups; this becomes the basic building block in laboratory design. Ordinarily one wants to build as much heterogeneity as possible into small-group composition, with the stipulation that there be enough commonality among participants so that any given participant can identify with at least one other person in the group. It is important to establish some home base within the learning experience, a place in which participants can experience support and safety and where they can attempt to integrate what they are learning about themselves. The intensive small-group experience becomes such a base in a laboratory.

Structured Experiences. A wide array of activities is available to the group facilitator as he begins planning a design (e.g., Pfeiffer & Jones, 1969 & 1974; 1970 & 1974; 1971 & 1974; 1973; 1975). Eleven major types of structured experiences are available: ice breakers, awareness expansion, interpersonal communication, intergroup communication, personal feedback, dyads, leadership, group process, group problem solving, competition, and organization development. Awareness expansion includes nonverbal exercises, graphic art exercises, dance and other body-expressive activities, sensory awareness and awakening experiences, fantasy, and drama ideas.

Any given activity may be equally appropriate in a personal growth design or in a laboratory focusing on leadership development, but since the goals of the two events may be significantly different, the processing of the data generated by the structured experience is decidedly different. For example, a structured experience that we have used from time to time in laboratories has been a checkerboard exercise.

The facilitator distributes materials and gives group members the task of organizing themselves to construct a checkerboard. In a basic human relations laboratory, the behavioral and feeling data that are generated by such an event would probably be processed in a T-group meeting, in which people would focus on their own emerging awareness and on their feelings and reactions to other people's behavior. They would be given feedback of a very personal nature about the effects of the process and the effects of each other's behavior. In a leadership development laboratory, the same event might be processed in terms of leadership styles that emerged during the event, styles of influence, roles people played, and decision-making procedures. There might also be an attempt to process the data in terms of theory of leadership. Structured experiences generate and focus data toward particular learning, but the major skill in their use is in adapting them to the particular learning needs of the participants in a given laboratory and in assisting participants in processing and integrating data that are generated by their use.

Lecturettes. The infusion of cognitive material into the laboratory experience is done in several ways. One may deliver brief lecturettes in large group sessions, commonly called "community" sessions. One may comment very quickly within an intensive small-group session about the theoretical implications of a particular set of behavioral data, one may provide a reading book prior to the laboratory experiences, or one may give handouts during the experience itself. The facilitator needs to develop a repertoire of brief lecturettes that he may use to highlight particular processes at any given time in the laboratory's development. The Lecturettes section of the *Annual* is intended to provide a resource for such brief theoretical inputs into laboratory design. In the laboratory itself, lecturettes may be used prior to particular learning experiences to provide a kind of cognitive map for the experience that is about to ensue, or they may be used to help focus the data from a particular structured experience or intensive group meeting. They provide a way of helping participants "make sense out of" the learning that they are experiencing and heighten the probability that the participant will relearn how to learn from his everyday experiences by providing him with cognitive models for guiding his behavior.

These brief lectures are aided considerably by visual presentations. Sometimes the use of a flip chart can make a particular lecturette easier to follow, and the outline of the lecturette can be posted for participants to read throughout the experience. A lecturette on the criteria of effective feedback, for example, can result in a poster listing such criteria, and, during the laboratory, participants can be guided in their giving and receiving feedback by a set of considerations that come to be internalized through the experience. Sometimes the posting of such theory material serves as a means of guiding participants' behavior without staff members having to remind them of particular learnings.

Instruments. Nonclinical measurement devices can be highly useful in a laboratory education design. They can serve to focus on particular behavioral science concepts and can provide a set of data whereby participants may explore themselves intra- and interpersonally, study group composition, and discover new behaviors in which they might consider engaging within the relative safety of the laboratory milieu. The Instrumentation section of the *Annual* is designed to provide easy access to instruments that might be incorporated into laboratory designs. Our usual style is to introduce an instrument by encouraging participants to be very open in responding to the items, to ask participants to complete the scale, to lecture on the rationale underlying the instrument, to illustrate the interpretation of the scoring by using our own scores for examples, and to have participants practice interpreting each other's scores (usually in helping pairs). We often follow this by posting the data to build norms for the particular laboratory and then processing the data in intensive small-group meetings that tend to focus on the personal relevance of the data at a relatively higher support level than characterizes individual interpretation. Instruments are not substitutes for experiential approaches, but they can often serve as highly effective means of focusing learning around a theoretical model.

These four basic components—intensive small groups, structured experiences, lecturettes, and instruments—can be varied almost infinitely to provide highly innovative, flexible designs to meet the learning needs of participants. In the next section we will deal with some major considerations within the laboratory itself to ensure that these components are utilized effectively.

GENERAL CONSIDERATIONS

Ten major considerations will be discussed in this section to guide the facilitator as he begins to converge on the process of designing a laboratory. This list of major dimensions constitutes a compilation of *dos* and *don'ts* for the process of designing.

Investment and Involvement. In designing a human-interaction laboratory, it is important for the facilitator to plan not to have passive audiences at any given time during the training event. Every participant needs to have something to do all the time during the formally planned sessions. If there is going to be a lecture, the facilitator will stress active listening. If he is using a structured experience, roles need to be assigned so that every person has something to do that contributes to his own learning within the context of that experience. The important thing is that from the very beginning each participant is led to accept the responsibility for his own learning within the laboratory context and that ample opportunity is given for him to act out his responsibility through participation.

Sequencing. Each activity within the laboratory should build from the previous sequence of activities and toward the next one. That is, every component of a laboratory design should fit into an ordered scheme that results in the attainment of the goals of the laboratory. The next section of this paper will contain a discussion of the unique sequencing concerns in personal growth and leadership development designs. Balancing should also be considered in the sequencing so that the participant does not get an overload of cognitive material. Even the meals should be strategically placed, and the effect of the interaction within the meals needs to be anticipated as one plans for the events that follow. Sometimes it is important in the sequence to have thematic material that runs throughout all the components of the laboratory design, processing a variety of events against the same theoretical model.

Content. It is highly desirable to use locally relevant content whenever possible. This is particularly true in leadership development laboratories, in which the content of the exercises needs to parallel closely the kinds of leadership concerns and problems that participants ordinarily face in their work. A number of data-generating techniques can be employed within the laboratory to ensure that the content of the learning designs is relevant to the participants as they are experiencing it. There are several useful strategies.

Participants can be asked to make notes to themselves about particular feelings that they are experiencing, thoughts that they are thinking, persons to whom they are reacting, and so on. One useful technique is the "think-feel" card, on which participants are to record their reactions at any particular point. On one side they are to write a sentence beginning with "I think," and on the other side they are to write a sentence beginning with "I feel." This process very often heightens participants' willingness to share these reactions with others.

A highly useful intervention in a group meeting or in other laboratory events is to form dyads and to ask each pair to interview each other with regard to their reactions to a particular issue, event, or piece of behavioral data at any given time. Often we ask people to use this as an exercise in active listening. Ordinarily the interviewer should not make notes but should paraphrase very often what he hears to make certain that he is not translating in terms of his own reality rather than being sensitive to the phenomenological system of the person being interviewed.

A list of concerns can be generated rapidly on a flip chart or chalkboard. Such a list may include issues facing the group at any given moment, problems facing the group, controversial topics, persons, etc. Participants can be asked to rank the list according to some criterion such as urgency or influence. Often it is useful to ask participants first to perform a ranking independently to establish their own point of view and then to divide into small groups to develop a consensus ranking of the material.

Questionnaires can be developed that include multiple-choice items, rating scales, open-end questions, and so on. These can be used prior to or within the laboratory to generate data for participant learning. It is important that participants take the responsibility to process the data, and it may be desirable to post the statistical results so that the group can analyze itself.

It is sometimes helpful for a group to look back on its own history to analyze how it has used its time quantitatively. A list of topics can be generated that have constituted the group's agenda in past meetings, and the amount of energy that has been expended on any given item can be discussed. Sometimes a group discovers that an inordinate amount of energy has been expended on particular concerns, and it may be able to use its time more efficiently.

Videotaping is an excellent technique. Often it is extremely difficult to recapture much of the data generated in a learning event depending on memory alone, and the advantages of videotape with instant and repeated playback are obvious. Nonverbal data can be highly focused by the use of this medium, and it is often very useful in teaching process awareness.

A group can look at its own development at any given moment through a problem-solving method called force-field analysis. A lecturette in the 1973 *Annual*, "Kurt Lewin's 'Force Field Analysis,'" describes this process.

Occasionally, teaching the distinction between content and process is made easier by using activities whose content is obviously a simulation of "real-world" concerns. When working with a group of persons in a laboratory setting, the task sometimes becomes so seductive that the group fails to look effectively at its own internal functioning. Such a process orientation can be generated rapidly by using an exercise such as the checkerboard to focus on interpersonal dynamics.

Processing. Perhaps our firmest commitment in laboratory design is to make absolutely certain that there is adequate time for processing the data that are generated by particular laboratory design components. It is in the processing activity itself, which immediately follows every learning experience, that the transfer of training is bolstered. If human relations training is, in fact, training for everyday work, then it is important that we heighten the probability that such transfer will take place. Processing refers to the talking through of behavioral and feeling data that emerge in a particular structured activity. We feel that it is both dangerous and unethical to leave large portions of data hanging that might be integrated in dysfunctional ways within the consciousness of a given individual. The importance of providing sufficient air time within the laboratory design to sort out and share reactions to particular events cannot be overemphasized. A number of structures have been developed to help participants in processing data. The following is a partial compendium of these designs.

Participants and facilitators can be used as observers in particular structured experiences. It is sometimes useful to provide process-observation recording forms on which the observer may make notes during the event. Sometimes we may interrupt an event to hear reports from the process observers. Occasionally we have several process observers who form a discussion panel after the event to pool their observations. In laboratories, we often incorporate into the design the option for any number of participants to take turns in functioning as external process observers. Occasionally we set up a particular structured experience in such a way that participants will stop at a predetermined point to process their reactions up to that point.

Facilitators may be used as consultants to a particular group accomplishing a task or working a given problem within a laboratory. This may be done on a continuous basis—that is, a consultant may be brought in while a group is working on a particular problem—or it may be that the timing of the interventions of the process consultant is preplanned. Laboratory participants can also be trained to perform this function.

After an activity on listening and process observation within a laboratory, participants can be encouraged to use each other as consultants in dyadic relationships that emerge during the laboratory. If two participants are having difficulty communicating with each other, they might seek out a third party to help them listen more effectively. This can be very useful training that can be transferred to the back-home situation. It is important for a participant to develop the ability to play the role of process consultant rather than to be a person who mediates conflict or takes sides on the content of a particular issue.

The group-on-group design is one of the most powerful processing designs with which we are familiar. What lends it potency is that a group operating within the fishbowl is under considerable pressure to work very hard at focusing on process. In addition, the group can use other participants as consultants for its own internal functioning.

To increase the air time for any given participant it is often useful to break up a large group into a number of small units of three to six for rapid processing of data. Sometimes we structure this so that there are reporters who will give brief synopses of the major themes of the subgroups to the total group at a predetermined time. Subgrouping performs the function of giving people a chance to be heard and understood very rapidly, and it can heighten the getting-acquainted process.

A circle of chairs can be placed in the center of the room with the ground rule that if an individual wishes to speak about what is occurring he must occupy one of the chairs in the center. This has the effect of including, during any given period, any number of participants in open interchange, and it is particularly useful when working with very large groups of people.

In looking back at the process of learning in the laboratory experience, sometimes participants can focus on particular things that they have been doing by developing contracts, or promises, with each other that they attempt to fulfill in the time remaining. Sometimes this process of contracting can lead to highly useful applications in the back-home setting. We sometimes incorporate within the helping-pair design the writing of contracts for back-home application of the learning process that a particular person has been experiencing, with planned follow-through built into the contract.

Pacing. It is important for the facilitator to keep things moving and to avoid passivity and boredom, but he must be sensitive to the effects of fatigue on the participants. One can design a laboratory that has such a break-neck pace that participants come out of the event having been overloaded with stimuli. Some time is needed for people to think things out, and free time needs to be built in simply to give people an escape from the heavy work demands of a laboratory.

As a general rule, when things begin to drag, it is probably time to make a change. Sometimes the most effective change is simply to point up the process that is emerging and to help participants understand its nature. In a group meeting, for example, if there is a long silence, it may be important for the group to deal with the responsibility of the individual participants to avoid dysfunctional quiet. If the pace is characterized by frequent interventions on the part of the facilitator, it may lead to dependency on the part of the participants and they may come to expect him to make things happen. The pace of the events within a laboratory, then, should be dictated by the probable fatigue effect, the necessity to provide plenty of time for adequate processing of data, and the need not to reinforce dependency on the staff.

Goals. As has been previously indicated, it is critical for the facilitator to know the priorities and learning goals of a particular laboratory, to be able to specify them clearly, and to be able to keep the learning event goal-directed. It is important that he also be able to help participants clarify their own goals if they are somewhat unclear. Every person in the laboratory should have some understanding of why he is there.

Voluntariness. A major goal of laboratory education is to increase freedom rather than to co-opt people into activities in which they otherwise might not participate voluntarily. This is especially true if persons attend the laboratory involuntarily. These individuals' participation in particular activities must be made voluntary. Some persons react with a great deal of tension to activities involving physical touch, and they should not be required or unduly coerced to participate in such exercises. The silent member of the intensive small group may be tyrannized by other group members into saying things that he does not want to reveal, and his voluntariness may be violated. Thus, in designing a laboratory, one must be sensitive to the needs of some participants not to involve themselves in every single activity.

Norms. The most meaningful expectations in the laboratory situation for the facilitator to establish and maintain are strategic openness, experimentation, and sensitivity to self and others. Strategic openness means avoiding the extremes of being dysfunctionally open or of colluding with other people not to talk about taboo topics. Experimentation means trying new behaviors within the laboratory situation. Sensitivity to self and others means that participants should be aware of the feelings that they are experiencing and that they should also attempt to be aware of the readiness of other people to get involved with them in open interchange of here-and-now data.

Data. Thoughts, feelings, and behavior are always present at any given point in the laboratory. Sometimes during a particular event participants may comment that nothing appears to be happening, but often this is simply evidence that they are not monitoring the complexity of the emerging process. The data-generating techniques that have been discussed previously can be highly effective in focusing particular here-and-now phenomena toward the learning goals of the laboratory.

Flexibility. The designer of the laboratory must plan to use maximum data from the event itself to modify the design so that it meets the learning needs of the participants. This means that he avoids "packaged" designs that are preplanned and that do not adequately account for the responsiveness of particular participants. We find it useful to overdesign laboratories in the sense that at any given point several options are being considered. This implies a lot of staffing time, especially if staff members are new to each other. In effect, this consideration of several options at any given point becomes a kind of on-the-job training for designing learning events.

SEQUENCING IN PERSONAL GROWTH AND LEADERSHIP DEVELOPMENT PROGRAMS

There is, we believe, an organic sequence of activities that is useful to consider in designing both personal growth and leadership development laboratories. The attempt in this section is to delineate this sequence in terms of the laboratory components previously discussed. The flow of activities within the two kinds of learning programs overlaps somewhat although the emphasis is often different; we believe that it is important to consider the design of these two kinds of laboratories because they are the most common types to be developed by group facilitators.

Personal Growth. The model for many personal growth laboratories has been based on the design, or lack of design, associated with two-week laboratories held in a retreat setting. Participants and staff would meet for the first time without an organized plan for activities, and together they would work through structuring a learning experience out of the ambiguities of an unstructured situation. A power vacuum would be artificially created by the phenomenon of the facilitators' refusal to accept responsibility for telling participants what to do. The typical participant response would be a series of "plop" statements, such as "Why don't we introduce ourselves?" Long periods of silence would be experienced, and after the frustration created by the situation reached a significantly high level, the group would begin to focus with varying degrees of hostility on the trainers. The comments would then tend to be "What are we supposed to be doing here? If they're paying you, they're paying you too much." The net result of this was that the group members would eventually come to accept that they were responsible for their own learning. On the way to that awareness, they would have resolved their issues around the power vacuum. This would inevitably include issues about leadership expectations, and frequently the plethora of feeling about authority figures would be opened up and discussed.

While the learnings inherent in dealing with the power vacuum were important, they consumed an inordinate amount of time when the design was translated to the weekend or weekly meeting models that have become more prevalent. Facilitators learned that what worked in a two-week design in the Maine woods does not necessarily work in a group that has a shorter lifetime. The training issue then becomes how to accelerate learning given restrictive time constraints. The use of structured experiences to focus on learning concepts, to generate learning data, and to accelerate the growth of group development and individual awareness signals the beginning of a set of solutions for the design dilemma.

In a personal growth laboratory, there are definite learning goals that involve the use of skills in their accomplishment; however, there is less emphasis on skill building than there is in the leadership development laboratory. The two key goals in personal growth are developing awareness of self and others and increasing skills in interpersonal relationships. Toward these ends, skills in listening, expressing, and responding are needed, and their development must be integrated into the design of the laboratory. These three skills will be discussed more thoroughly when an account of all of the skills necessary for leadership development is made. This is one of the areas in which these two basic laboratory concepts overlap.

The sequence of events leading to the optimum use of time in fostering the learning goals in personal growth can be developed from the flow of learning that is implied in the following tabulation. The intent here is to spell out a series of things that need to be done in the laboratory in a logical flow, from getting acquainted to going home. This sequence is relevant both to retreats and to spaced meetings. A variety of structures can be utilized to effect this sequence. This is not the design of an ideal laboratory so much as it is an outline of the learning needs of participants during a personal growth laboratory.

1. *Getting Acquainted.* The major need at the beginning of the laboratory is for participants to establish some familiarity with each other, so that the initial caution with which people interact can be eased. The unfreezing process begins in the initial stages of the laboratory. A variety of getting-acquainted designs is available in the literature on structured experiences in human relations training.

2. *Closing Expectation Gaps.* It is important that the goals of the laboratory experience be made explicit and that they be correlated with the goals of participants. It is equally important that participants and staff have a clear understanding of what each expects of the other. The most difficult training situation that we know of exists when participants expect one kind of experience and staff members expect something else. Under this condition there needs to be immediate negotiation and clarification of assumptions.

3. *Legitimizing Risk Taking.* Early in the laboratory experience, it is significant for participants to test their willingness to know and to be known by other people, to express their feelings, to explore how other people are reacting to them, and to attempt new ways of behaving in relation to other people. At this point it is important that risk taking be legitimized and reinforced as a norm in the laboratory setting.

4. *Learning About Feedback.* Soon after the beginning of the laboratory experience, it is useful to provide some kind of instruction in the feedback process so that effective sharing can be heightened in the intensive, small-group sessions and in the free time between formally planned sessions. Lecturettes, structured experiences, instruments, and trainer interventions can serve to provide an atmosphere in which feedback becomes expected and experienced freely. These methods can also introduce some conceptual models that might guide participants in the sharing of information about each other.

5. *Developing an Awareness of Process.* After the intensive small group in a personal growth laboratory has had a brief history, it is often highly useful to begin to explore the dynamic processes that are emerging in the development of the group. This may be done through a fishbowl procedure or a variety of other designs previously discussed. The group can grow more rapidly if it stops occasionally in the interaction among members to process the kinds of patterns that are beginning to emerge in its development.

6. *Integrating Conceptual Models.* Transfer of training is more likely to be achieved if participants receive assistance in integrating the behavioral and affective data of the laboratory experience through looking at some theoretical models of personal and group development. This may be done through the use of instruments, lecturettes, demonstrations, and so on.

7. *Experimenting with Self-Expression.* Growth in awareness of self and others can be heightened through the use of expressive techniques, such as nonverbal exer-

cises and fantasies. Toward the middle of the laboratory experience, it is often useful to build into the design some opportunity for people to "stretch" their personal development through the use of symbolic self-expression.

8. *Planning Back-Home Application.* Ideally, plans for back-home application begin to develop from the beginning of the laboratory. For example, an early experience that is often useful is a goal-setting activity, with reassessment in the middle and at the end of the laboratories. Often we use role playing, contracting, and helping pairs for applying learnings of the laboratory to particular back-home situations. Toward the end of the experience, considerable effort should be placed on getting participants to accept responsibility for making definite plans for changes that they want to institute after the laboratory is over. These plans need to be evaluated in the light of some criteria for application, and this evaluation is often best done in collaboration with one or two other individuals with whom the participant feels comfortable.

9. *Assisting Re-Entry.* Closure activities in a personal growth laboratory should enable the participant to move back into his ordinary environment with a minimal amount of difficulty. Activities that emphasize feeling and cause participants to be "high" can result in dysfunctional re-entry into the immediate back-home situation. It is important to assist participants in exploring the observation that they are full of consciousness of themselves. At this point they are far more sensitive to their feelings and are more willing to be involved with people in open, trusting ways than are their "real-life" associates who have not just spent a comparable amount of time in a personal growth laboratory.

This general sequence does not imply a rigid structure. It is simply an attempt to highlight the needs of participants to develop an ability to talk with each other, to learn how to make sense out of the interaction that is occurring, and to heighten the development of ways that participants can use the experience in their everyday existence.

Leadership Development. Another genre of training events has been known by a number of euphemistic titles. One often sees labels such as "dynamics of leadership," "management development," "executive development," and "communication skills," and the events themselves are sometimes publicized as conferences, workshops, laboratories, or seminars. Thematic in these training events is a focus on skill building and conceptual development through experiential methods. They differ from personal growth laboratories more in degree than in kind; that is, there is a comparatively higher degree of emphasis on skill building and comparatively lower emphasis on growth in awareness of feelings about self and others. There is also a comparatively higher degree of structure within the design and a liberal use of simulations within the laboratory setting.

The skills that are being learned during a leadership development laboratory are multifarious. They include listening, expressing, responding, participating, collaborating, facilitating, observing, intervening, reporting, and conceptualizing. The skills that we discuss first are the ones that receive the most attention in the laboratory, and those toward the end receive comparatively less emphasis. This is, of course, a very subjective ranking of their criticalness within the training program.

Listening is a basic communication skill, and it is reinforced throughout the laboratory experience through structured activities and through the process of paraphrasing within intensive small-group meetings. Expressing one's thoughts and feelings is worked on through nonverbal exercises, through process-reporting exercises, through intensive group meetings, etc. Responding to the communication of others is the third basic communication skill that is reinforced during the leadership training laboratory. The intent in working on this skill is to get people to develop a heightened awareness of and sensitivity to the persons to whom they are responding, so that they are able to communicate within a system that has meaning to others.

Leaders need to know how to be followers because following is a part of leading. Participating in group activities in which the "leader" is simply one of a group of people working shoulder-to-shoulder is an important skill to focus on during the laboratory experience. In developing skill in collaborating, participants are encouraged to learn how to use conflict functionally and to avoid conflict-reducing techniques, such as horse-trading, in order to determine the best judgment of the group in solving problems. Leaders need to develop the ability to facilitate other people's growth by encouraging them to take responsibility for the task that faces the group. Some skill building is needed in defining leadership as the facilitation or the sharing of responsibility.

When observing, leaders need to be able to see the complexity of intra-individual, interindividual, intragroup, and intergroup phenomena, so some skill development is planned within the laboratory to help leaders learn about the behavioral manifestations of interpersonal dynamics. Closely related to observing is the skill in using what one sees to help a group to improve its own internal functioning by learning about its ongoing process. Leaders need to develop the consultation skill of process intervention. In addition, leaders need skills in reporting or summarizing large batches of group content in order to provide succinct accounts of what has been decided.

Conceptualizing is perhaps the most complex of leadership skills. This involves looking at human interaction from a theoretical point of view. Conceptual models can be incorporated into leadership development laboratories in such a way as to allow the leaders to develop their own theories of leadership.

The following sequence is, we believe, an organic, logical, and effective flow of activities that need to take place in leadership development laboratories. Again, this sequence is proposed as relevant whether the laboratory takes place over a weekend or during a semester-long course.

1. *Getting Acquainted.* Here the basic need is to infuse a note of psychological safety into the proceedings by familiarizing participants with each other and with staff members on a personal level. The effort is to create a climate in which people can have easy access to each other. It is important in the beginning of such laboratories for people to be able to establish their credentials. Often participants feel a strong need to impress people with who and what they are.

2. *Closing Expectation Gaps.* In a leadership development laboratory, as in a personal growth laboratory, it is important that the goals of the laboratory experience be made explicit and correlated with the goals of participants. It is equally important that participants and staff have a clear understanding of what each expects of the other. If the facilitator determines that there is a wide expectation gap, he must immediately negotiate to close it.

3. *Roles and Shared Leadership.* The concept of roles and functions of different group members and the notion of dynamic, shared leadership is introduced. This sets the tone for using theoretical material in an experiential format to focus on ourselves as leaders in relation to other people.

4. *Learning About Feedback.* Soon after the beginning of the laboratory experience, it is useful to provide instruction in the feedback process so that effective sharing can be heightened. Lecturettes, structured activities, instruments, and trainer interventions can serve to provide an atmosphere in which feedback becomes expected and experienced freely.

5. *Developing an Awareness of Process.* After the leadership development laboratory has had a brief history, it is highly useful to begin to explore the dynamic processes emerging in the group. This may be done through a fishbowl procedure or a variety of other designs previously discussed. The group can develop effectively if it stops occasionally in the interaction among members to process the kinds of leadership and roles that are beginning to emerge.

6. *Competition Task.* Early in a leadership development laboratory we introduce an activity that is likely to result in participants' exploring the functional and dysfunctional effects of interpersonal competition. Sometimes a competitive atmosphere is established deliberately, such as in an intergroup model-building activity, or it may arise spontaneously in a relatively unstructured task experience.

7. *Collaboration Task.* It is useful to follow a competitive experience with an activity in which people are expected to attempt deliberately to collaborate with

other people on a task. We want to demonstrate that collaboration is possible within a culture that rewards a competitive spirit.

8. *Consensus Task.* Closely related to the collaboration task is consensus seeking. Many structured experiences can be chosen from the point of view of involving a number of people in arriving at collective judgments that are superior to individual judgments. What we attempt to illustrate in this kind of experience is the concept of synergy.

9. *Planning Back-Home Application.* Toward the end of the laboratory experience it is important for participants to begin making definite plans for particular behaviors that they want to experiment with and/or change in their back-home leadership situation. It is sometimes useful to have participants write themselves letters about what they are going to attempt to change based on both cognitive material and their own experience during the lab.

In addition to a sequence of activities fostering skill building and the development of a set of leadership concepts, some material is thematic throughout a leadership-development laboratory design. Three concepts need to be stressed during the laboratory itself: process awareness, criteria of effective feedback, and theories of leadership. The design of the leadership development laboratory in general, then, consists of encouraging participants to experiment with leadership phenomena, involving them in a series of activities to explore leadership from the point of view of looking at themselves in roles, looking at group effects and the dynamics of competition and collaboration, and planning the transfer of learning to the leadership situation back home.

PROFESSIONAL DEVELOPMENT IN DESIGNING LABORATORIES

Building a Repertoire. The facilitator who wants to improve his ability to design personal growth and leadership development laboratories can take a number of steps toward such growth. The first thing that he can do to develop his skills is to build a repertoire of materials that he can use in his design work. He can familiarize himself with structured experiences and instruments available for use in training, and he can store within his head any array of lecture materials that he can call on at a moment's notice to explain particular phenomena in the laboratory setting.

Co-Facilitating. A second step that he can take to improve his ability to design laboratories is actively to seek opportunities to work with a variety of other facilitators. This has a number of important advantages. First, he can receive concentrated, highly specific feedback on his style as a facilitator; he can improve his ability to diagnose participants' needs; and he can spend staff time critiquing the design and debriefing laboratories after they are completed. This, we believe, is the best professional-development strategy that is currently available. There is no substitute for experience with other trained professionals working in a laboratory setting with live participants.

Varying Clients. A third step that the facilitator can take is seeking out opportunities to work with various client groups. This requires him to be flexible in design and to avoid developing design packages that may be irrelevant to the learning needs of particular clients. There are obvious ethical restrictions on the facilitator as he seeks out clients. Since human relations training is generally considered to be a professional-level activity, professional ethics require him not to overrepresent his qualifications. But within ethical restrictions, the facilitator can grow professionally by generating experience in working with a variety of participants.

Studying Designs. Another activity that can result in professional development in designing laboratories is studying other facilitators' designs. This is a somewhat controversial subject in that, within the field of laboratory education, there is a tendency for facilitators to be closed and possessive about the designs that they have developed. It is not uncommon for facilitators to conclude that they have developed a program that is highly salable, and often one encounters reluctance to share designs with other professionals. What has happened within this field, then, is the systematic violation of a norm that we try to sell to clients—that is, to be open and collaborative. University Associates conducted a life-planning laboratory some time ago in which over half the participants attended primarily to learn how to conduct the laboratory themselves. We renamed the event the "rip-off lab," and we had a good laugh about it. What was significant about that experience was the fact that, before the laboratory began, the participants' hidden agenda was a taboo topic. We made it an open subject and legitimized it so that people would not feel the need to conceal their motives from the lab staff. In studying other facilitators' designs, it is important that the design not be accepted *in toto*. Others' designs are almost always, in some aspect, irrelevant to the particular needs of another client system. Adaptation should be the keynote.

Attending Workshops. A fifth step that the group facilitator can take to develop himself in the area of design is to attend professional-development workshops. Many learning experiences are available for the behavioral science consultant that afford him opportunities to obtain supervised practice in the design of laboratories. Various training organizations, such as National Training Laboratories and University Associates, offer such professional-development programs.

Attending Labs as Participants. Finally, it is highly useful for facilitators to attend laboratories occasionally as participants rather than as staff members. The human element is the critical point with regard to effective facilitation. The most significant ethical boundary impinging on the facilitator is the need to remain healthy: not to deceive himself about who he is, what he is up to, where he is going, and so on. Participating in laboratories as a participant means living by the same kind of values that we are attempting to teach other people and continuing to develop our ability to provide experiences that offer meaningful human contact with other people. The major need in staff development is to integrate one's personal and professional development. Personal growth is necessary but not sufficient; that is, even though the facilitator may be a highly effective person, he still needs the technology of laboratory education in order to be effective in fostering other people's development.

What we have attempted in this paper is to spell out some of the learnings about the process of designing laboratories for the enhancement of personal growth and leadership development so that facilitators can explore this task more straightforwardly and creatively. We continue to stress the norm that such ideas be shared by facilitators in the field.

REFERENCES

Blake, R., & Mouton, J. S. The instrumented training laboratory. In I. R. Weschler & E. M. Schein (Eds.), *Selected readings series five: Issues in training.* Washington, D.C.: National Training Laboratories, 1962, pp. 61–85.

Buchanan, P. C., & Reisel, J. Differentiating human relations training laboratories. *Social Change*, 1972, 2, 1–3.

Jones, J. E. Types of growth groups. In J. W. Pfeiffer & J. E. Jones (Eds.), *The 1972 annual handbook for group facilitators.* La Jolla, Ca.: University Associates, 1972.

Pfeiffer, J. W., & Jones, J. E. (Eds.). *A handbook of structured experiences for human relations training* (Vols. I, II, III, IV, and V). La Jolla, Ca.: University Associates, 1969 & 1974; 1970 & 1974; 1971 & 1974; 1973; 1975.

INTRODUCTION TO STRUCTURED EXPERIENCES

Structured experiences—designed to focus on individual behavior, constructive feed-back, processing, and psychological integration—are infinitely varied and variable. They can easily be adapted to the particular needs of the group, the aim of a training design, or the special competencies of the facilitator. In publishing structured experiences, we assume that facilitators are, by their nature, innovators. As one friend remarked, "I use your materials all the time, but I almost never do things the way you guys describe them."

Since the expertise of individual facilitators varies, we have arranged the structured experiences in the *Annuals* and the *Handbooks* in order of the degree of understanding, skill, and experience required by the facilitator. The first structured experiences generate less affect and data than do later ones, thus demanding much less background of the facilitator to use them effectively and responsibly.

We are concerned that all human relations training experiences have adequate processing so that the participants are able to integrate their learning without the stress generated by unresolved feelings or a lack of understanding. It is here that the expertise of the facilitator becomes crucial. If the structured experience is to be responsive to the needs of the participants, the facilitator must be able to assist participants in successfully processing the data that emerge from that experience. Thus, he should select an activity on the basis of two criteria—his own competence and the participants' needs.

CONSIDERATIONS IN DEVELOPING A STRUCTURED EXPERIENCE

To further the creation and availability of these valuable materials, we are including some points and questions to be considered when developing a structured experience.

Goals. These should be limited in number and stated in language that participants can understand. A good goal is *specific*, not general; it is *performance oriented*, to guide the person toward what he is going to *do*; it *involves* the individual in his goal objective; it is *observable*, so that other people can see the result; and, most important, it is *realistic*. For maximum effectiveness, a goal must be attainable.

Group Size. The minimum and maximum number of participants, the optimum size of the group, and the number and size of subgroups should be noted where relevant. If there are extra participants, how should they be utilized? (They could, for example, be designated as observers or be added to subgroups.)

Time Required. This should be a realistic expectation, based on actual trials of the experience. If the experience requires a long period of time, can it be divided into more than one session?

Materials. The criteria here are easy availability, utility, and uncomplicated preparation. The specific forms, sheets of information, or worksheets needed and the quantities of each should be listed. If appropriate, an observer sheet should be devised for the activity. Audio-visual aids (such as felt-tipped pens, newsprint, sound or film equipment, etc.), pencils and paper, and any other special materials should be indicated if applicable.

Physical Setting. What are the participants' needs: Must groups be private, quiet, isolated? Do participants sit around tables or lie on the floor? Do they need writing surfaces? Can the experience take place outdoors? Do rooms need to be specially designated or arranged for certain groups or subgroups? Easily movable furniture is usually desirable to aid in the flexibility of the group.

Process. This is a step-by-step procedure that should indicate what the facilitator *does* and *says* and what the participants *do* in the appropriate sequence. The beginning and end of each step should be specified. A time estimate may be useful for each step or phase.

Variations. Adaptations may be noted to vary the activity's content, sequence, use of observers, time for each step, materials, size of groups, complexity of process, and use with intact groups.

References. If and when relevant, similar structured experiences, lecturette sources, or background reading should be indicated.

Credit Line. Ideas and designs of others should be acknowledged; if there is more than one author to be credited, authors' names should be given in the order of the significance of their contributions, the senior author or contributor listed first.

Worksheets. These should be designed and written so that they have sufficient room in which the participants may write; are simple and easy to reproduce; have clear instructions; and are necessary and meaningful to the activity. Wherever possible, each worksheet should be on one page, with type large enough to read easily. It is practical to have the worksheet contain its own instructions. If it does not, it should tell the participant that the facilitator will give oral instructions. Sources for worksheets should be acknowledged.

Handouts. This format is especially useful for a discussion of the theory underlying new behavior suggested by the structured experience. Unless necessary, participants should not be allowed to read handout materials while the process is running. However, if handouts are to be provided, participants should be told at the beginning of the experience so that they will not have to take notes.

CONSIDERATIONS IN USING A STRUCTURED EXPERIENCE

Certain questions need to be asked by the facilitator who is contemplating using a structured experience as an intervention in a training event. This set of considerations constitutes a self-examination that is intended to help the facilitator select and develop designs that are both relevant and effective.

What are the goals of this group and why was it formed? Structured experiences are designed for a variety of purposes, but their most effective use is within programs that are aimed at specific learning goals. The facilitator needs to keep these goals in mind constantly.

At what stage is the group in its development or what stage is it likely to reach? Different issues surface at various stages of group development and some activities are particularly useful at some points in group life. A feedback design may be inappropriate in the earliest stages but highly beneficial after the group has a brief history.

What is my contact with the group? Some groups expect the facilitator to "run" everything. It is important to minimize the gap in expectations between the facilitator and the participants. Using too many structured experiences may reinforce dependency on the part of the members, and they may turn to the facilitator to introduce an activity rather than confronting their own behavior. The facilitator needs to make it clear that each member is responsible for his own learning.

Why is it important that I intervene? Because it is possible for the facilitator to meet his needs at the participants' expense, it is important that he assess his own motives for intervening into the interaction among members. Useful distinctions may be made between making things happen, letting things happen, and being a part of what is happening. One useful thought is "When in doubt, wait."

Why does this particular intervention appeal to me? It may be that the structured experience seems appropriate because it would be "fun" to do, but the overriding consideration should be the learning needs of the participants at a particular point in the group's development. One should be careful not to overuse any given activity; this might indicate that the facilitator has "a solution in search of a problem."

How ready are these participants to take risks, to experiment? Some structured experiences, such as guided fantasies and nonverbal activities, are threatening to many participants and may evoke anxiety and defensiveness, rather than openness to learning. It is useful, however, to establish an experimentation norm in laboratory education, and participants should be expected to "stretch" somewhat.

What content modifications can I make for an effective, appealing design? Local issues and concerns can be incorporated into structured experience materials and processes in order to heighten the possibility of the transfer of training. Such advance preparation can have a high payoff in developing work norms and avoiding "game playing." Roles, goals, company policies, issues, cases, etc., can be gathered with the help of participants.

What advance preparations need to be made? Appropriate rooms, with the right kinds of furniture and equipment, need to be scheduled. The staff may need to be prepared. Materials have to be duplicated and assembled. Sometimes it is helpful to prearrange the furniture so that participants are seated in preparation for the first phase of the process.

How rigid are the time restraints for the session? It is necessary not to generate more data than can be adequately processed within the session. It is better not to use an activity than to leave too much data "hanging" at the end. One consideration is to anticipate which elements of the design can be speeded up or expanded, if necessary.

How am I going to set up the processing? Since the processing of the data generated by the structured experiences is more important than the experience itself, this planning phase should be carefully considered. A number of strategies can be used, such as process observers who have been briefed and who are using comprehensive guides; lecturettes; instrumented processing with brief questionnaires; subgrouping; the empty chair or group-on-group techniques; interviewing. Some of the data may be saved for use in later training designs.

How am I going to evaluate the effectiveness of the design? Since structured experiences are best employed in an atmosphere directed toward specific goals, some assessment of the extent to which the goals of a given activity were met is necessary. Such a study may be impressionistic and/or "objective," but it needs to be planned beforehand. The facilitator needs to decide the basis for judging whether or not or to what degree the aims of a particular intervention were accomplished.

FAILURE OF STRUCTURED EXPERIENCES

Structured experiences can "fail." That is, they may not produce the predicted results, or they may produce unexpected results.

Usually, such failure occurs when the experiential model is truncated or abbreviated or when it is inadequately implemented. Each step in the model is an essential part of the entire sequence; each needs sufficient attention to effect its full impact. Inadequate processing is the most common cause of the failure of the model.

Unfortunately, failure on the part of any facilitator only increases the chances that other facilitators may encounter difficulty in their attempts to present a structured experience. If participants in a learning activity have previously had ineffective training experiences, it is likely that they will be more resistant to, and less inclined to involve themselves in, such experiences in the future.

Thus, the question of the "failure" of structured experiences becomes significant. Failure promotes subsequent failure. For this reason, we are stressing here the need for facilitators to confront the demands and requirements of the experiential model so that they—and their colleagues who follow them—may gather the rewards and benefits the model offers.

The implications of the model stress the necessity for adequate planning and sufficient time for each step. An appropriate structure is especially important for processing, generalizing, and applying. When handled with care, concern, and skill, the experiential approach is invaluable for group facilitators in the human relations training field.

NUMBERING OF STRUCTURED EXPERIENCES

The structured experiences are numbered consecutively throughout the series of *Handbooks* and *Annuals,* in order of publication of the volumes. The following list specifies the numbers of the structured experiences to be found in each publication in the Pfeiffer and Jones Series in Human Relations Training.

Structured Experience	Publication
1 through 24	Volume I, *Handbook*
25 through 48	Volume II, *Handbook*
49 through 74	Volume III, *Handbook*
75 through 86	1972 *Annual*
87 through 100	1973 *Annual*
101 through 124	Volume IV, *Handbook*
125 through 136	1974 *Annual*
137 through 148	1975 *Annual*
149 through 172	Volume V, *Handbook*

CLASSIFICATION OF STRUCTURED EXPERIENCES

Each of the 172 structured experiences published in the five volumes of the *Handbook* and the four volumes of the *Annual* is categorized by type and then listed in numerical sequence within each category. (See the list on the previous page that indicates the order of publication of the structured experiences.) The categories are as follows:

> Ice Breakers
> Awareness Expansion
> Interpersonal Communication
> Intergroup Communication
> Personal Feedback
> Dyads
> Leadership
> Group Process
> Group Problem Solving
> Competition
> Organization Development.

Classifying these materials is somewhat arbitrary, since they can be adapted for a variety of training purposes. Although any given experience could belong to a number of classifications, we have listed each only once, categorizing it in the area of its *most probable* use.

ICE BREAKERS

Number	Title [Author]	Goals	Time Required	Volume & Page No.
1	Listening and Inferring: A Getting-Acquainted Activity	To facilitate the involvement of individuals in a newly formed group	Fifteen minutes	I-3
2	Two-Four-Eight: Building Teams	To divide a large group into workable subgroups in such a way as to increase group cohesiveness and identity	Approximately thirty minutes	I-5
5	Who Am I?: A Getting-Acquainted Activity	To allow participants to become acquainted quickly in a relatively non-threatening way	Approximately forty-five minutes	I-19

ICE BREAKERS (Continued)

Number	Title [Author]	Goals	Time Required	Volume & Page No.
25	Group Conversation: Discussion-Starters [D. Castle]	To develop a compatible climate and readiness for interaction in a group through sharing personal experience	Can be a fifteen-minute preface to other group activities or planned for an entire meeting	II-3
27	Jigsaw: Forming Groups	To establish group cohesion by forming a large number of participants into groups with pre-determined compositions	Approximately thirty minutes	II-10
42	First Names, First Impressions: A Feedback Experience [J. E. Jones]	To get acquainted with other members of a small group; to discover one's initial impact on others; to study phenomena related to first impressions—their accuracy and effects	Approximately one hour	II-88
49	"Who Am I?" Variations: A Getting-Acquainted Activity	To allow participants to become acquainted quickly in a relatively non-threatening way	Approximately forty-five minutes	III-3
87	Peter-Paul: Getting Acquainted [E. L. Solley]	To help group members get acquainted quickly in a relatively nonthreatening manner; to explore feelings generated by "becoming another person"; to explore the dimensions of a brief encounter; to emphasize the need for careful, active listening during conversation	Minimum of ten minutes plus two minutes per group member	'73-7
88	"Cold" Introductions: Getting Acquainted [J. E. Jones]	To help participants to get to know each other while building expectations of risk taking and receptivity to feedback; to build norms of openness, experimentation, and attention to process	Approximately three minutes per participant	'73-9

ICE BREAKERS (Continued)

Number	Title [Author]	Goals	Time Required	Volume & Page No.
96	Participant-Staff Expectations [A. H. Munoz]	To provide participants and facilitators the opportunity to examine and discuss mutual expectations and perceptions regarding the training program; to reduce the "expectation gap" between participants and facilitators	Approximately one hour	'73-29
101	Getting Acquainted: A Potpourri	To be used as ice breakers in human relations training events	Varies with each listed experience	IV-3
125	Hum-Dinger: A Getting-Acquainted Activity [A. D. Duncan]	To break a large group into smaller groups in a non-threatening manner; to facilitate contact between all members of a large group in a related climate of fun and humor	Approximately thirty minutes	'74-7
149	Energizers: Group Starters	To prepare participants for meetings	Varies with each activity	V-3

AWARENESS EXPANSION

Number	Title [Author]	Goals	Time Required	Volume & Page No.
16	Fantasies: Suggestions for Individuals and Groups	To promote heightened awareness of self and others	Varies with each fantasy	I-75
19	Awareness Expansion: A Potpourri	To heighten one's sensory awareness	Varies with each activity	I-86
20	Graphics: Self-Disclosure Activities	To generate self-disclosure data through graphics	Varies with each activity	I-88

AWARENESS EXPANSION (Continued)

Number	Title [Author]	Goals	Time Required	Volume & Page No.
22	Nonverbal Communication: A Collection of Activities	To learn new ways of expressing one's feelings, independent of one's vocabulary; to express feelings authentically using nonverbal symbolism; to focus on nonverbal symbolism; to focus on nonverbal cues that one emits	Varies with each activity	I-101
44	Nonverbal Communication: A Collection	To learn new ways of expressing one's feelings, independent of one's vocabulary; to express feelings authentically using nonverbal symbolism; to focus on nonverbal cues that one emits	Varies with each activity	II-94
46	Life Planning: A Programmed Approach	To apply concepts of planned change to an individual's personal, interpersonal, and career development	Six hours split into three two-hour periods	II-101
47	Microlab: A Training Demonstration	To demonstrate human relations training methods; to accelerate the development of growth-producing norms, such as openness and attention to feelings	Depends on variations employed in the design	II-113
56	Feelings and Defenses: A Spontaneous Lecture	To study feelings significant to group members and defenses they use; to help group members take responsibility for their own learning	About thirty minutes	III-31
65	Think-Feel: A Verbal Progression [J. E. Jones]	To make distinctions between thoughts and feelings; to learn to link feeling feedback to observable behavior; to practice empathizing	Forty-five minutes	III-70
71	Lemons: A Sensory-Awareness Activity	To increase sensory awareness	One hour	III-94

AWARENESS EXPANSION (Continued)

Number	Title [Author]	Goals	Time Required	Volume & Page No.
72	Nonverbal Communication: A Collection	To learn new ways of expressing one's feelings, independent of one's vocabulary; to express feelings authentically using nonverbal symbolism; to focus on nonverbal cues that one emits	Varies with each activity	III-97
74	Personal Journal: A Self-Evaluation	To heighten participants' awareness of the sequence of events and the corresponding emotional development which takes place in a laboratory or a workshop; to aid in self-disclosure	Any number of periods of ten to fifteen minutes each, depending on the design of the laboratory or workshop	III-109
75	Frustrations and Tensions	To help participants to become aware of their responses to tense, frustrating situations; to study alternative responses to such situations	Approximately forty-five minutes	'72-5
84	Psychomat	To provide an atmosphere in which participants can encounter each other in a variety of ways; to encourage creative, sensitive risk taking on the part of participants; to explore reactions to a highly unstructured interpersonal situation	Six to nine hours	'72-58
85	Growth and Name Fantasy [A. G. Banet, Jr.]	To provide group participants with an opportunity to review, in fantasy, the phases of growth and development they have accomplished; to review their sense of individual identity	Approximately forty-five minutes	'72-59
89	Gunnysack: An Introduction to Here-and-Now [J. E. Jones]	To establish the norm of attending to here-and-now data and "gunnysacking" then-and-there data; to help participants to become aware of their own here-and-now reactions	Approximately thirty minutes	'73-11

AWARENESS EXPANSION (Continued)

Number	Title [Author]	Goals	Time Required	Volume & Page No.
90	Make Your Own Bag: Symbolic Self-Disclosure [C. Lawson]	To raise levels of trust and openness in a group; to make group members aware of themselves and others as persons	Approximately one hour and forty-five minutes	'73-13
119	Group Exploration: A Guided Fantasy [L. Berman]	To allow individuals to share their means of coping with fear and stress as well as their personal responses to pleasure	Approximately one hour	IV-92
122	Expressing Anger: A Self-Disclosure Exercise [G. R. Gemmill]	To study styles of expressing anger in a group setting; to study effects of anger in a group setting; to legitimize the presence and expression of anger within groups; to identify behaviors which elicit anger in others; to explore ways of coping with anger	Approximately forty-five minutes	IV-104
128	Re-Owning: Increasing Behavioral Alternatives [H. B. Karp]	To assist participants in exploring aspects of themselves that they might not be presently aware of or may be underutilizing; to extend the range of behavioral alternatives open for effective communication	Approximately one hour	'74-18
136	Relaxation and Perceptual Awareness: A Workshop [J. L. Hipple, M. Hutchins, & J. Barott]	To learn basic techniques of physical relaxation, breathing processes, and self-awareness; to experience one's physical state of existence and personal perceptions of inner and outer reality and fantasy	Three hours	'74-84
137	What Do You See?: A Discovery Activity [A. G. Kirn]	To expand awareness of those things that have meaning for life and work; to discover new areas of individual relevance and interest; to promote changing negative thinking to positive thinking	A minimum of one hour	'75-7

AWARENESS EXPANSION (Continued)

Number	Title [Author]	Goals	Time Required	Volume & Page No.
142	**Live Case:** A Group Diagnosis [R. K. Conyne & D. H. Frey]	To illustrate problems involved in overgeneralizing; to practice interviewing techniques as a method of generating data about an individual; to study the process of forming hypotheses from available information	Approximately two hours	'75-40
143	**Ideal Cards:** A Self-Disclosure Activity [B. P. Holleran]	To encourage interaction and self-disclosure about ideals; to reveal group members' priorities for their ideals	Approximately one and one-half hours	'75-43

INTERPERSONAL COMMUNICATION

Number	Title [Author]	Goals	Time Required	Volume & Page No.
4	**One-Way, Two-Way:** A Communications Experiment [*adapted from H. J. Leavitt*]	To conceptualize the superior functioning of two-way communication through participatory demonstration; to examine the application of communication in family, social, and occupational settings	Approximately forty-five minutes	I-13
7	**Broken Squares:** Nonverbal Problem-Solving	To analyze some aspects of cooperation in solving a group problem; to sensitize participants to behaviors which may contribute toward or obstruct the solving of a group problem	Approximately forty-five minutes	I-25
8	**Listening Triads:** Building Communications Skills	To develop skills in active listening; to study barriers to effective listening	Approximately forty-five minutes	I-31
28	**Rumor Clinic:** A Communications Experiment	To illustrate distortions which may occur in transmission of information from an original source through several individuals to a final destination	Thirty minutes	II-12

INTERPERSONAL COMMUNICATION (Continued)

Number	Title [Author]	Goals	Time Required	Volume & Page No.
41	Status-Interaction Study: A Multiple-Role-Play [J. W. Pfeiffer]	To explore effects of status differences and deference on interaction among group members	Forty-five minutes	II-85
50	Behavior Description Triads: Reading Body Language	To practice describing nonverbal behavior objectively, without interpretation; to study the body-language messages that accompany verbalization; to alert group members to the variety of signals they use to communicate	Approximately fifteen minutes	III-6
52	Not-Listening: A Dyadic Role-Play [H. B. Karp]	To allow participants to experience the frustration of not being heard; to promote listening readiness	Approximately thirty minutes	III-10
76	Quaker Meeting	To generate a large number of ideas, suggestions, approaches to a problem or topic when the group is too large to employ brainstorming techniques; to gather data quickly for a large group to process	Fifteen minutes for the actual "Quaker meeting" plus processing time appropriate for the particular group	'72-11
86	Symbolic Closing Exercise [M. Smith]	To finish a workshop or laboratory with a sense of closure; to re-enact the group process in symbolic nonverbal action	Approximately ten minutes	'72-61
91	Perception of Task: A Teaching-Learning Exercise [R. T. Williams]	To examine how perceptions of a learning task by teacher and learner influence teaching styles and learning styles	One hour	'73-15
93	Building Open and Closed Relationships [adapted from W. Barber]	To enable group members to focus on the elements of relationships which characterize them as open or closed; to facilitate the cohesiveness of personal growth or otherwise-designated groups who will be working together	One and one-half to two hours	'73-20

INTERPERSONAL COMMUNICATION (Continued)

Number	Title [Author]	Goals	Time Required	Volume & Page No.
108	**Ball Game:** Controlling and Influencing Communication [R. D. Jorgenson]	To explore the dynamics of assuming leadership in a group; to increase awareness of the power held by the member of a group who is speaking at any given time; to diagnose communication patterns in a group	Approximately thirty minutes	IV-27
110	**Organization Structures:** Communication Patterns [T. Irwin]	To demonstrate the varying effectiveness of different organization structures; to diagnose working relationships within an intact group; to illustrate less efficient modes of communication; to illustrate perceived alienation	Approximately one hour	IV-34
112	**The "T" Test:** An Experiential Lecture on Traits [A. J. Reilly]	To introduce the concept of personality traits; to illustrate the process of inferring characteristics from behavior; to help diminish some of the unproductive anxiety which is often associated with filling out psychological instruments or inventories	Approximately thirty minutes	IV-41
121	**Toothpicks:** An Analysis of Helping Behaviors [R. R. Middleman]	To identify differing approaches to assisting others in a task; to explore the effects of the various helping approaches on task accomplishment and interpersonal relations	Approximately one hour	IV-99
138	**Party Conversations:** A FIRO Role-Play [C. L. Kormanski]	To experiment with different types of interpersonal behavior; to demonstrate the concepts in Schutz's theory of interpersonal relations	Approximately two and one-half hours	'75-10

INTERPERSONAL COMMUNICATION (Continued)

Number	Title [Author]	Goals	Time Required	Volume & Page No.
152	Helping Relationships: Verbal and Nonverbal Communication [C. G. Carney]	To demonstrate the effects of posturing and eye contact on helping relationships; to focus group members' attention on the impact of their nonverbal behaviors on other individuals; to teach basic nonverbal listening and attending skills	Approximately thirty minutes	V-13
153	Babel: Interpersonal Communication [P. M. Ericson]	To examine language barriers, which contribute to break-downs in communication; to demonstrate the anxieties and frustrations that may be felt when communicating under difficult circum-stances; to illustrate the impact of nonverbal com-munication when verbal communication is ineffec-tive and/or restricted	Approximately two hours	V-16

INTERGROUP COMMUNICATION

Number	Title [Author]	Goals	Time Required	Volume & Page No.
33	Hollow Square: A Communications Experiment [W. H. Schmidt & A. Shedlin]	To study dynamics involved in planning a task to be carried out by others; to study dynamics involved in accomplishing a task planned by others; to explore both helpful and hindering com-munication behaviors in assigning and carrying out a task	Approximately one hour	II-32
62	Polarization: A Demonstration [J. E. Jones & J. J. Jones]	To explore the experience of interpersonal polariza-tion—its forms and effects; to study conflict manage-ment and resolution	Approximately two hours	III-57

INTERGROUP COMMUNICATION (Continued)

Number	Title [Author]	Goals	Time Required	Volume & Page No.
63	Discrimination: Simulation Activities	To simulate the experience of discrimination; to study phenomena of stereotyping people	Varies with each activity	III-62
95	**Sex-Role Stereotyping** [M. Carson]	To make distinctions between thoughts and feelings about sex-role stereotyping; to examine one's own reactions to sexism in a mixed group; to link feeling feedback to observable behavior; to avoid over-generalization; to explore the experience of interpersonal polarization— its forms and effects; to study conflict resolution	Approximately two hours	'73-26
120	**Dimensions of Trust:** A Symbolic Expression [J. Costigan]	To explore the various dimensions and meanings of trust; to promote the creative expression of trust	Approximately one hour	IV-96
158	**Absentee:** A Management Role Play [R. J. Carpenter, Jr.]	To explore the dynamics of decision making; to study the resolution and management of conflict; to reveal loyalty patterns among peers and superiors	Approximately one and one-half hours	V-49

PERSONAL FEEDBACK

Number	Title [Author]	Goals	Time Required	Volume & Page No.
13	Johari Window: An Experience in Self-Disclosure and Feedback	To introduce the concept of the Johari Window; to permit participants to process data about themselves in terms of self-disclosure and feedback	Approximately two hours	I-65
17	Leveling: Giving and Receiving Adverse Feedback [J. W. Pfeiffer].	To let participants compare their perceptions of how a group sees them with the actual feedback obtained from the group; to legitimize giving negative feedback within a group; to develop skills in giving negative feedback	Approximately ten minutes per participant	I-79
18	Dependency-Intimacy: A Feedback Experience [J. E. Jones]	To provide instrumented feedback; to study how the personal dimensions of dependency and intimacy affect group development	Approximately one and one-half hours	I-82
23	Coins: Symbolic Feedback [J. William Pfeiffer]	To experiment with giving feedback symbolically; to share feelings involved with giving, receiving, and rejection	Approximately one and one-half hours	I-104
38	Role Nominations: A Feedback Experience [based on K. D. Benne & P. Sheats]	To provide feedback to group members on the roles fellow members see them playing; to study various types of roles in relation to group goals; to demonstrate that leadership in a small group consists of several functions which should be shared among members	Approximately one and one-half hours	II-72
43	Verbal Activities Within Groups: A Potpourri	To be used as openers when meetings of the groups are infrequent, or may be used as interventions within meetings	Varies with each activity	II-91

PERSONAL FEEDBACK (Continued)

Number	Title [Author]	Goals	Time Required	Volume & Page No.
57	Nominations: Personal Instrumented Feedback	To provide feedback to group members on how they are perceived by each other; to analyze the climate and the norms of the group by studying members' behavior, composition of the group, and members' expectations of each other	Approximately one hour	III-33
58	Peer Perceptions: A Feedback Experience [J. E. Jones]	To let each group member know to what degree he is seen to be similar to each other member; to study feeling reactions to being considered "different"; to help each member define the dimensions of human similarity and dissimilarity he believes are important	Two to three hours	III-41
97	Puzzlement: A "Mild" Confrontation [R. R. Kurtz]	To help participants confront each other's behavior in helpful ways; to stimulate the amount of feedback given and received in a group; to share the feelings involved in giving and receiving feedback	Approximately one and one-half hours	'73-30
99	Analyzing and Increasing Open Behavior: The Johari Window [P. G. Hanson]	To describe open and closed behavior in terms of the Johari Window; to identify facilitating and inhibiting forces which affect the exchange of feedback; to encourage the development of increased open behavior in the group through facilitated feedback	Approximately two and one-half hours	'73-38

PERSONAL FEEDBACK (Continued)

Number	Title [Author]	Goals	Time Required	Volume & Page No.
100	Motivation: A Feedback Exercise [D. F. Michalak]	To learn the concepts in Maslow's Need Hierarchy; to get feedback on one's use of motivational techniques in terms of Maslow's Need Hierarchy	At least one-half hour	'73-43
104	The Gift of Happiness: Experiencing Positive Feedback [D. Keyworth]	To promote a climate of trust, self-worth, and positive reinforcement within a small group; to experience giving and receiving positive feedback in a nonthreatening way	Approximately five minutes per participant and about thirty minutes for processing	IV-15
106	Sculpturing: An Expression of Feelings [L. A. McKeown, B. Kaye, R. McLean, & J. Linhardt]	To provide a nonverbal medium for the expression of feelings toward another person; to promote feedback on individual behavior	Approximately forty-five minutes	IV-21
107	The Portrait Game: Individual Feedback [F. Maire]	To allow participants to receive a composite feedback picture from the members of their group as a departure from single-source individual feedback; to provide an opportunity for participants to compare their individual perceptions of how the group is experiencing their behavior with the reality of the group's experience	A minimum of twenty minutes per participant	IV-24

PERSONAL FEEDBACK (Continued)

Number	Title [Author]	Goals	Time Required	Volume & Page No.
109	Growth Cards: Experimenting with New Behavior [M. Cahn]	To develop an accepting atmosphere for risk taking and self-disclosure; to give those within a larger laboratory community a legitimate entry point for the provision of individual feedback to participants in other groups; to supply participants with specific, individual feedback to aid them in making decisions concerning an agenda for modifying their own behavior; to increase understanding and acceptance of personality components which decrease interpersonal effectiveness; to strengthen individual commitment to behavioral change through open verbalization and the development of a method or prescription for modification; to reinforce group skills of decision making and task performance	Approximately two hours	IV-30
123	Stretching: Identifying and Taking Risks [R. R. Kurtz]	To help participants become aware of interpersonal behavior which is risky for them; to increase participants' awareness of the relationship between risk-taking behavior and the attainment of personal growth goals; to encourage risk-taking behavior as a way of expanding participants' behavioral repertoire	Approximately two hours	IV-107

PERSONAL FEEDBACK (Continued)

Number	Title [Author]	Goals	Time Required	Volume & Page No.
129	Forced-Choice Identity: A Self-Disclosure Activity [J. J. Sherwood]	To gain insight about oneself; to facilitate self-disclosure and feedback; to encourage community-building; to enhance enjoyment of the group experience through a change-of-pace activity	Approximately two hours	'74-20
146	Payday: A Closure Activity [R. L. Bunning]	To provide for self- and group evaluation of each participant's performance within the group; to allow each participant to compare his self-evaluation with the group's evaluation of him; to give participants experience in evaluating others in a constructive, concrete manner	Approximately one hour	'75-54
167	Cups: A Power Experience [A. J. Reilly]	To increase awareness of the meanings of power; to experience giving, receiving, and not receiving power	Approximately two hours	V-111
168	Adjectives: Feedback [J. E. Jones]	To help participants clarify values that apply to human relationships; to establish the norms of soliciting and giving both positive and negative feedback	Approximately one hour	V-114
170	Person Perception: Feedback [R. H. Dolliver]	To provide feedback to individual group members about how they are perceived by others; to help participants clarify what underlies their tendency to categorize other persons	Approximately one hour	V-131

DYADS

Number	Title [Author]	Goals	Time Required	Volume & Page No.
21	Dyadic Encounter: A Program for Developing Relationships [J. E. Jones & J. J. Jones]	To explore knowing and trusting another person through mutual self-disclosure and risk taking	A minimum of two hours	I-90
45	Helping Pairs: A Collection	To build helping relationships ancillary to small-group experiences; to give participants an opportunity to try out new behavior within a dyadic relationship; to provide group members with ways of checking out their perceptions of and reactions to laboratory experiences	Varies with each activity	II-97
70	Intimacy Program: Developing Personal Relationships [*adapted from S. M. Jourard*]	To accelerate the getting-acquainted process in groups; to study the experience of self-disclosure; to develop authenticity in groups	Approximately one and one-half hours	III-89
116	Dialog: A Program for Developing Work Relationships [J. E. Jones & J. J. Jones]	To increase openness in work relationships; to generate higher trust in interpersonal relations in work settings; to clarify assumptions that persons who work together make about each other and each other's jobs	A minimum of two hours	IV-66
169	Dyadic Renewal: A Program for Developing Ongoing Relationships [C. A. Kelley & J. S. Colladay]	To periodically explore various aspects of a relationship through mutual self-disclosure and risk taking	A minimum of two hours	V-116

LEADERSHIP

Number	Title [Author]	Goals	Time Required	Volume & Page No.
3	**T-P Leadership Questionnaire:** An Assessment of Style [*adapted from Sergiovanni, Metzcus, & Burden*]	To evaluate oneself in terms of task orientation and people orientation	Approximately forty-five minutes	I-7
9	**Committee Meeting:** Demonstrating Hidden Agendas [*based on J. Gold & L. Miller*]	To illustrate the effects of hidden agendas on task accomplishment in a work group	Approximately one and one-half hours	I-36
14	**Conflict Resolution:** A Collection of Tasks	To generate data about how groups resolve conflict	Varies with each activity	I-70
34	**Hampshire In-Basket:** A Management Activity [J. W. Pfeiffer]	To discover general management principles through personal involvement with problem solving; to examine one's management style; to plan applications of management principles	Approximately three hours	II-41
59	**Line-Up and Power Inversion:** An Experiment	To expand the individual's awareness of his influence on the group; to experience power inversion	Approximately one and one-half hours	III-46
60	**Dividing the Loot:** Symbolic Feedback	To provide symbolic feedback to participants; to explore the responsibilities and problems of leadership	One hour	III-49
127	**Leadership Characteristics:** Examining Values in Personnel Selection [C. L. Kormanski]	To compare the results of individual decision making and group decision making; to explore values underlying leadership characteristics; to examine effects of value judgments on personnel selection	Approximately two hours	'74-13

LEADERSHIP (Continued)

Number	Title [Author]	Goals	Time Required	Volume & Page No.
130	Conflict Fantasy: A Self-Examination [J. A. Stepsis]	To facilitate awareness of strategies for dealing with conflict situations; to examine methods of responding to conflict; to introduce the strategy of negotiation and to present the skills required for successful negotiation	Approximately forty-five minutes	'74-22
154	Styles of Leadership: A Series of Role Plays [G. M. Phillips]	To explore the impact that leaders have on decision making in groups; to demonstrate the effects of hidden agendas	Approximately two hours	V-19
159	Fork-Labyrinth: Leadership Practice [J. F. Veiga]	To diagnose the behavior of leaders and followers in a small group performing a complex competitive task; to teach "on-line" feedback and coaching on leadership behavior; to practice different leadership behaviors	Approximately three hours	V-53
162	Pins and Straws: Leadership Styles [H. L. Fromkin]	To dramatize three general styles of leadership: autocratic, laissez-faire, and democratic; to increase awareness of how different styles of leadership can affect the performance of subordinates; to study the phenomenon of competition among groups	Approximately two hours	V-78

GROUP PROCESS

Number	Title [Author]	Goals	Time Required	Volume & Page No.
6	Group-On-Group: A Feedback Experience	To develop skills in process observation; to develop skills in giving appropriate feedback to individual group members	Approximately one hour	I-22
10	Process Observation: A Guide	To provide feedback to a group concerning its process; to provide experience for group members in observing process variables in group meetings	Minimum of ten minutes for processing	I-45
24	Assumptions About Human Relations Training: An Opinionnaire [J. E. Jones; worksheets by J. Dickinson, C. Dee, J. E. Jones, & B. H. Arbes]	To allow the group to assess the degree to which it has consensus on a number of assumptions that underlie laboratory learning; to assist co-facilitators in identifying each other's biases about training; to discover some possible "blind spots" that the training staff may have about training	Minimum of one hour	I-107
26	Miniversity: Sharing Participants' Ideas	To provide for dissemination of information, using participants as resources, during a conference, workshop, or institute	Time is dependent on the size of the group, the facilities available, and the number of "courses" offered	II-7
37	Self-Interaction-Task: Process Observation Guides [J. E. Jones]	To practice observing small-group process; to gain experience in reporting process observations to a group; to provide instrumented feedback on one's interpersonal orientations	Two hours	II-68
39	Group Development: A Graphic Analysis [J. E. Jones]	To compare the development of a small group along the dimensions of task functions and personal relations; to compare members' perceptions of the developmental status of a group at a given time	Approximately forty-five minutes	II-76

GROUP PROCESS (Continued)

Number	Title [Author]	Goals	Time Required	Volume & Page No.
48	**Process Intervention:** A Facilitator Practice Session	To provide practice in intervening in small groups; to generate feedback on intervention styles	At least one hour	II-115
51	**Empty Chair:** An Extended Group Design	To allow all participants to become involved voluntarily in a group-on-group experience when the size of the total group makes discussion impractical	Open	III-8
55	**Group Self-Evaluations:** A Collection of Instruments	To help a group evaluate its own functioning; to provide a way to examine objectively the participation of group members; to explore the norms that have developed in a group which has been meeting for some time	Varies according to the evaluative procedures used	III-22
79	**What to Look For in Groups:** An Observation Guide [P. G. Hanson]	To assist group members in understanding and being more perceptive about group process	Three hours	'72-19
92	**Medial Feedback:** A "Mid-Course Correction" Exercise	To generate evaluative data about the effects of a laboratory education design while there is still time to modify it; to study group process phenomena both as a participant and as an observer	Approximately one and one-half hours	'73-17
113	**Growth Group Values:** A Clarification Exercise [O. Elliott & D. Zellinger]	To clarify one's own value system; to explore values held in common within a group; to study differences existing between groups; to begin to remove stereotypes held by members of different groups	Approximately one and one-half hours	IV-45
114	**Closure:** Variations on a Theme	To be useful in closing human relations training events; can also be employed to foster self-disclosure in personal growth groups	Varies with each idea	IV-49

GROUP PROCESS (Continued)

Number	Title [Author]	Goals	Time Required	Volume & Page No.
124	The In-Group: Dynamics of Exclusion [G. Goldberg]	To allow participants to experience consciously excluding and being excluded; to confront feelings which exclusion generates; to examine processes by which social identity is conferred by the excluding group and accepted by the excluded member	Approximately one and one-half hours	IV-112
126	Cog's Ladder: A Process-Observation Activity [G. O. Charrier]	To enhance awareness of factors which distinguish process from content in group interaction; to explore a model of group development	One hour	'74-8
135	Kidney Machine: Group Decision-Making [G. M. Phillips]	To explore choices involving values; to study problem-solving procedures in groups; to examine the impact of individuals' values and attitudes on group decision making	Approximately one hour	'74-78
139	Faculty Meeting: A Multiple Role-Play [F. H. McCarty & B. Nisenholz]	To study behaviors that facilitate and that block communication in groups; to explore the effects of process feedback on team functioning	Approximately two and one-half hours	'75-15
148	Group Leadership Functions: A Facilitator-Style Activity [R. K. Conyne]	To explore four basic leadership functions of group facilitators; to study the relationship between leadership functions and general interpersonal style	Approximately two hours	'75-63
172	Group Composition: A Selection Activity [G. M. Phillips & A. G. Banet, Jr.]	To explore the process of selection of group members; to assist facilitators in identifying their biases about group composition; to study similarities and differences between personal growth and psychotherapy groups	Approximately one and one-half hours	V-139

GROUP PROBLEM SOLVING

Number	Title [Author]	Goals	Time Required	Volume & Page No.
11	**Top Problems:** A Consensus-Seeking Task [J. J. Sherwood]	To compare the results of individual decision making with the results of group decision making; to teach effective consensus-seeking behaviors in task groups	Approximately one and one-half hours	I-49
12	**Choosing a Color:** A Multiple-Role-Play [J. W. Pfeiffer]	To explore behavioral responses to an ambiguous task; to demonstrate the effects of shared leadership	Approximately forty-five minutes	I-56
15	**Residence Halls:** A Consensus-Seeking Task	To study the degree to which members of a group agree on certain values; to assess the decision-making norms of the group; to identify the "natural leadership" functioning in the group	Approximately one hour	I-72
29	**Group Tasks:** A Collection of Activities	To be used in studying group process	Varies with each activity	II-16
30	**NORC:** A Consensus-Seeking Task [J. E. Jones]	To compare results of individual decision making and of group decision making; to generate data to discuss decision-making patterns in task groups	Approximately one hour	II-18
31	**Lutts and Mipps:** Group Problem-Solving [*based on Rimoldi*]	To study the sharing of information in a task-oriented group; to focus on cooperation in group problem solving; to observe the emergence of leadership behavior in group problem solving	Approximately forty-five minutes	II-24
53	**Brainstorming:** A Problem-Solving Activity	To generate an extensive number of ideas or solutions to a problem by suspending criticism and evaluation; to develop skills in creative problem solving	Approximately one hour	III-14

GROUP PROBLEM SOLVING (Continued)

Number	Title [Author]	Goals	Time Required	Volume & Page No.
64	**Kerner Report:** A Consensus-Seeking Task	To compare the results of individual decision making with the results of group decision making; to generate data to discuss decision-making patterns in task groups; to diagnose the level of development in a task group	Approximately one hour	III-64
69	**Supervisory Behavior/ Aims of Education:** Consensus-Seeking Tasks *[worksheets adapted from D. Nylen, J. R. Mitchell, & A. Stout]*	To explore the relationships between subjective involvement with issues and problem solving; to teach effective consensus-seeking behaviors in task groups	Approximately one and one-half hours	III-84
77	**Twelve Angry Men Prediction Task**	To compare the accuracy of predictions based upon group consensus seeking to those made by individuals; to generate data for a discussion of the merits of attempting consensus	Approximately two and one-half hours	'72-13
80	**Energy International:** A Problem-Solving Multiple Role-Play	To study how task-relevant information is shared within a work group; to observe problem-solving strategies within a group; to explore the effects of collaboration and competition in group problem solving	Approximately two hours	'72-25
94	**Traditional American Values:** Intergroup Confrontation	To clarify one's own value system; to explore values held in common within a group; to study differences existing between groups; to begin to remove stereotypes held by members of different groups	Approximately one and one-half hours	'73-23

GROUP PROBLEM SOLVING (Continued)

Number	Title [Author]	Goals	Time Required	Volume & Page No.
98	**Strategies of Changing:** A Multiple-Role-Play [D. J. Marion & A. Edelman; *based on R. Chin & K. D. Benne*]	To acquaint people with three different interpersonal strategies for trying to effect change in human systems	Approximately one hour	'73-32
102	**Shoe Store:** Group Problem-Solving [A. M. Zelmer]	To observe communication patterns in group problem solving; to explore interpersonal influence in problem solving	Thirty to sixty minutes	IV-5
103	**Joe Doodlebug:** Group Problem-Solving [*adapted from M. Rokeach*]	To explore the effect of participants' response sets in a group problem-solving activity; to observe leadership behavior in a problem-solving situation	Approximately forty-five minutes	IV-8
115	**Consensus-Seeking:** A Collection of Tasks [worksheets by D. Keyworth, J. J. Sherwood, J. E. Jones, T. White, M. Carson, B. Rainbow, A. Dew, S. Pavletich, R. D. Jorgenson, & B. Holmberg]	To teach effective consensus-seeking behaviors in task groups; to explore the concept of synergy in reference to outcomes of group decision making	Approximately one hour	IV-51
117	**Pine County:** Information-Sharing [L. Dunn]	To explore the effects of collaboration and competition in group problem solving; to study how task-relevant information is shared within a work group; to observe problem-solving strategies within a group; to demonstrate the impact of various leadership styles on task accomplishment	Approximately one hour	IV-75

GROUP PROBLEM SOLVING (Continued)

Number	Title [Author]	Goals	Time Required	Volume & Page No.
133	Farm E-Z: A Multiple-Role-Play, Problem-Solving Experience [J. L. Joyce]	To study the sharing of information in task-oriented groups; to learn to distinguish a true problem from those which are only symptomatic; to observe problem-solving strategies within a group	Approximately two hours	'74-44
134	Hung Jury: A Decision-Making Simulation [S. C. Iman, B. D. Jones, & A. S. Crown]	To study decision-making processes	Approximately two hours	'74-64
140	Lost at Sea: A Consensus-Seeking Task [P. M. Nemiroff & W. A. Pasmore]	To teach the effectiveness of consensus-seeking behavior in task groups through comparative experiences with both individual decision making and group decision making; to explore the concept of synergy in reference to the outcomes of group decision making	Approximately one hour	'75-28
141	Nominal Group Technique: An Applied Group Problem-Solving Activity [D. L. Ford, Jr.; *adapted from* A. Delbecq & A. Van de Ven]	To increase creativity and participation in group meetings involving problem-solving and/or fact-finding tasks; to develop or expand perception of critical issues within problem areas; to identify priorities of selected issues within problems, considering the viewpoints of differently oriented groups	Two hours	'75-35
151	Cash Register: Group Decision Making [*based on* W. V. Haney]	To demonstrate how decision making is improved by consensus seeking; to explore the impact that assumptions have on decision making	Approximately thirty minutes	V-10

GROUP PROBLEM SOLVING (Continued)

Number	Title [Author]	Goals	Time Required	Volume & Page No.
155	Sales Puzzle: Information Sharing [*adapted from A. A. Zoll III*]	To explore the effects of collaboration and competition in group problem solving; to study how information is shared by members of a work group; to observe problem-solving strategies within a group	Approximately one hour	V-34
156	Room 703: Information Sharing [J. R. Joachim]	To explore the effects of collaboration and competition in group problem solving; to study how task-relevant information is shared within a work group; to observe group strategies for problem solving	Thirty to forty-five minutes	V-39
157	Letter Occurrence/ **Health Professions Prestige:** Consensus-Seeking Tasks [K. D. Scott & J. W. Pfeiffer]	To compare decisions made by individuals with those made by groups; to teach effective consensus-seeking techniques; to demonstrate the phenomenon of synergy	Approximately one hour per task	V-44

COMPETITION

Number	Title [Author]	Goals	Time Required	Volume & Page No.
32	**Model-Building:** An Intergroup Competition	To study interpersonal and intergroup competition phenomena; to explore the feeling content and behavioral results of winning and losing; to provide feedback to group members on their contributions in a task situation	Approximately one and one-half hours	II-29
35	**Auction:** An Intergroup Competition [J. W. Pfeiffer]	To explore relationships between leadership and decision making in a competitive situation; to illustrate effects of task success or failure on the selection of group representatives and leaders	Approximately one hour	II-58
36	**Win As Much As You Can:** An Intergroup Competition [*based on W. Gellerman*]	To dramatize the merits of both competitive and collaborative models within the context of intragroup and intergroup relations; to illustrate the impact of win-lose situations	Approximately one hour	II-62
54	**Towers;** An Intergroup Competition	To study phenomena of competition among groups; to explore the feeling content and behavioral outcomes of winning and losing; to provide a basis for feedback to group members on their relations with other group members and their productivity in a task situation	Approximately one and one-half hours	III-17
61	**Prisoners' Dilemma:** An Intergroup Competition	To explore trust between group members and effects of betrayal of trust; to demonstrate effects of interpersonal competition; to dramatize the merit of a collaborative posture in intragroup and intergroup relations	Approximately one hour	III-52

COMPETITION (Continued)

Number	Title [Author]	Goals	Time Required	Volume & Page No.
78	Unequal Resources	To provide an opportunity for observing group use of resources which have been distributed unequally; to observe bargaining processes	Approximately one hour	'72-17
81	Intergroup Model-Building: **The Lego Man** [W. B. Reddy & O. Kroeger]	To extract the learnings from a competitive teamwork experience, in terms of leadership style, developing alternatives, dominance and submission within teams, and distribution of work and resources; to diagnose the dynamics of an intact group in terms of role taking	Approximately two hours	'72-36
82	Greeting Cards: An Organization Simulation	To observe a group's organizational style and functioning; to gather data on individuals' responses to creating and operating a production-centered organization; to give group members feedback on their organizational behavior	Three to six hours	'72-44
83	Decisions: An Intergroup Negotiation [H. I. Feir, with R. J. Turner, R. Cox, D. N. Kanouse, & R. G. Mason]	To experience the issues surrounding intergroup trust building and trust betrayal; to explore considerations of intergroup competition versus collaboration; to examine limited communication under stress; to study negotiation and negotiation strategies; to consider group decision-making processes	A minimum of four and one-half hours	'72-51

COMPETITION (Continued)

Number	Title [Author]	Goals	Time Required	Volume & Page No.
105	Wooden Blocks: A Competition Exercise [A. M. Zelmer]	To explore individual and small group goal-setting behavior and achievement motivation; to study interpersonal and intergroup competition phenomena; to explore feelings and outcomes of winning and losing	Approximately one hour	IV-18
147	World Bank: An Intergroup Negotiation [N. H. Berkowitz & H. A. Hornstein]	To experience the conflict between advantages of co-operation and advantages of competition in a mixed-motive dilemma; to explore some dynamics of trust between groups; to practice negotiation skills	Approximately three hours	'75-56
150	Riddles: Intergroup Competition [B. P. Holleran]	To observe competitive behavior among groups; to determine how a group interacts with other groups when it is dependent on them for the completion of its task	Approximately one and one-half hours	V-5
160	Tinkertoy Bridge: Intergroup Competition [G. Bellman]	To analyze individual and team actions in relation to on-the-job experiences; to build awareness of the need for teamwork in completing a task; to demonstrate the effects of competition on team efforts	Approximately one and one-half hours	V-60
161	Lego Bridge: Intergroup Competition [P. Mumford]	To observe spontaneous patterns of organization in work groups; to explore the relationship between planning and production; to study the effects of intergroup competition on team functioning	Approximately one and one-half hours	V-73
163	Coloring Book: An Organization Experiment [*based on M. J. Miller*]	To explore relationships between organizational design and task complexity	Approximately one and one-half hours	V-85

COMPETITION (Continued)

Number	Title [Author]	Goals	Time Required	Volume & Page No.
164	Testing: Intergroup Competition [P. R. Scholtes]	To explore the impact of the lack of communication in competitive situations; to demonstrate the need for collaboration and interdependence	Approximately one and one-half hours	V-91
165	Marbles: A Community Experiment [*adapted from* *F. L. Goodman*]	To study community from the perspectives of establishing, enforcing, and interpreting rules; to explore rule-governed behaviors	Approximately two hours	V-98

ORGANIZATION DEVELOPMENT

Number	Title [Author]	Goals	Time Required	Volume & Page No.
40	Force-Field Analysis: Individual Problem-Solving [*based on* *W. G. Bennis &* *S. Eisen*]	To study dimensions of problems and to devise strategies for solving them through diagram and analysis; to experience the consultative role	Approximately two and one-half hours	II-79
66	Team-Building: A Feedback Experience	To help an intact work group diagnose its functioning; to establish a co-operative expectation within a task group; to assist a "real-life" group or business manager (leader, chairman, supervisor) to develop norms of openness, trust, and inter-dependence among team members and/or members of his organization	A minimum of one day	III-73
67	Organizational Mirror: A Feedback Experience	To generate data that can permit an organization to diagnose its functioning; to establish avenues of feedback between an organization and other groups with which it is linked	Approximately two hours	III-78

ORGANIZATION DEVELOPMENT (Continued)

Number	Title [Author]	Goals	Time Required	Volume & Page No.
68	Intergroup Meeting: An Image Exchange	To improve the relationship between two groups, such as levels of management, groups, males and females; to explore how groups interact with each other	Three hours	III-81
73	Wahoo City: A Role Alternation [P. Lawson]	To experience the dynamics of an alternate, unaccustomed role in a situation of community (or organization) conflict; to develop skills in conflict resolution, negotiation, and problem solving; to introduce process analysis and feedback as necessary community (or organization) development techniques	A minimum of two hours	III-100
111	System Problems: A Diagnostic Activity [M. S. Perlmutter & C. R. Ahrons]	To generate data about the functioning of an intact group or a growth group; to diagnose the way a system approaches problem solving	Approximately one hour	IV-38
118	Twenty-Five Questions: A Team Development Exercise [J. E. Jones]	To enhance work relationships in intact groups; to stimulate group discussion about work-related topics; to clarify assumptions that team members make about each other	Approximately one and one-half hours	IV-88
131	Roxboro Electric Company: An OD Role-Play [H. Thomson, with B. Bell, M. Brosseau, P. Fleck, & E. Kahn]	To provide an experience in sensing organizational problems; to provide feedback on interviewing effectiveness; to explore organizational diagnosis and action planning	Approximately two and one-half hours	'74-24
132	Planning Recommendations or Action: A Team-Development Guidebook [R. P. Crosby]	To study the process of group decision making; to explore action planning	Approximately three hours	'74-32

ORGANIZATION DEVELOPMENT (Continued)

Number	Title [Author]	Goals	Time Required	Volume & Page No.
144	**Lindell-Billings Corporation:** A Confrontation Role-Play [T. H. Patten, Jr.]	To provide an opportunity to practice confrontation; to explore design considerations in using confrontation inside an organization; to examine and develop skills in intergroup conflict, negotiation, and problem solving	Approximately three hours	'75-46
145	**Win What, Lose What?** An Intergroup Conflict Intervention [K. Finn]	To examine the elements of intergroup conflict; to illustrate a process of conflict resolution	Approximately three hours	'75-51
166	**Agenda Setting:** A Team-Building Starter [J. E. Jones]	To create and rank-order an agenda for a team-building session; to generate ownership of and commitment to commonly perceived problems facing a work group; to develop effective listening skills	Approximately one hour	V-108
171	**Role Clarification:** A Team-Building Activity [J. E. Jones]	To clarify both expectations that team members have of others' roles and conceptions that team members have of their own roles; to promote renegotiation of role responsibilities within a work unit; to teach a process of role adjustment that can become a work-group norm	A minimum of three hours	V-136

INTRODUCTION TO INSTRUMENTS

Instruments can be used in a number of ways by group facilitators. Data from inventories can be interpreted normatively or intrapersonally, but it is important that they be coordinated carefully with the goals of the training design. Some uses of instrumentation include the following:

Providing instrumented feedback to group members. Participants complete, score, and interpret their own scales. They can be asked to predict each other's scores. They can fill out scales for each other as feedback.

Manipulating group composition. For brief, experimental demonstrations of the effects of group composition, various mixes of group members can be established. Long-term groups can be built that offer the promise of beneficial outcomes. Extremes of both homogeneity and heterogeneity can be avoided.

Teaching theory of interpersonal functioning. Some brief instruments are intended primarily to introduce concepts. Participants are involved with theory by investing in an activity such as completing an inventory related to the model being explored.

Researching outcomes of training interventions. Even scales with relatively low reliability can be effective in the study of group phenomena when used with pretest or follow-up procedures.

Studying here-and-now process in groups. It is sometimes helpful to use an instrument to assist the group in diagnosing its own internal functioning. The data can be focused on what is happening and what changes are desirable.

DISADVANTAGES AND ADVANTAGES OF USING INSTRUMENTS[1]

It is important to note both the advantages and the disadvantages in using instruments in human relations training.

Disadvantages

One of the key disadvantages of using instruments is that people often fear that someone has, so to speak, obtained an indelible fingerprinting of them, that they have been exposed, that somebody has gotten into their mind and tapped it. It is important for

---

[1]The following discussion on the disadvantages and advantages of using instruments is taken from J. William Pfeiffer and Richard Heslin, *Instrumentation in Human Relations Training*, La Jolla, Ca.: University Associates, 1973, pp. 11–17.

facilitators using instruments to reduce this tendency to overstate the accuracy and stability of an instrument.

Another disadvantage is that instruments tend to encourage participants to be dependent on the facilitator, thus locating the leadership (control) of the group with the facilitator rather than allowing it to be shared among the members.

The use of instruments can be a means of dissipating the useful tension of person-to-person encounter, especially in a personal growth workshop. Both the participants and the leader may be denied some of the ambiguous but potentially growth-inducing tension produced by face-to-face encounter and reactions to one another.

Instruments often generate a rash of nit-picking responses in which the participants question the items, reliability, validity, or relevance of an instrument. Much valuable time can be used in arguing about the instrument itself. Nit-picking is often a result of the fact that the participant has received information that disturbs him, and he has a tendency to fear that this profile is irrevocably "him" or that people are going to interpret his data in a negative fashion.

Instruments also have the potential of generating significant hostility from participants who may see them as irrelevant, time consuming, and, in general, diverting attention from the key issues of the workshop. This may be attributable in part to a preconceived notion that "structure" is not an appropriate part of group experience, particularly in a personal growth group.

Finally, instruments can supply a person with more feedback than he is ready to handle; that is, an instrument can overload him with information that he does not have time to assimilate, to work through, to put into perspective.

Avoiding the Disadvantages

A number of the disadvantages mentioned can be avoided by removing the mysticism surrounding instruments. Effort should be made to prevent people from assuming that an instrument is an error-free, God-directed opening of the soul to everyone. Rather, participants should be encouraged to view instrumented experiences like any other choice-making experience in their everyday lives. They have given answers to a lot of situations described in the instrument, added up those answers, and come up with a score. If they have trouble understanding where the score came from they should be encouraged to go back to each item fed into the score, examine how they responded to each item and how they scored it, and perhaps compare their responses to other people's—item by item, response by response, and situation by situation.

A second way of avoiding some of the disadvantages of instruments is to make sure that individuals have sufficient time to process what the instrument has revealed about them. They should be given an opportunity to talk through their scores, to compare their scores in detail with those of others in the group, and to discuss why they see life from a different perspective than some of the other participants. They may also discuss how their view of their score reflects their personal orientation and compare this with some other people's orientations.

Advantages

Instrumented approaches give a recipient early opportunities to understand the theory involved in the dynamics of his own group situation—an understanding that will increase his involvement. By judicious choice of an appropriate instrument during the first group session, the facilitator can quickly offer the participant a theory about personality style, group development, interpersonal relations, or leadership that he can use throughout the rest of the group experience.

Another advantage of using instruments is that they give the person some constructs and terminology early in the group experience that he can use in looking at his and other people's behavior and in categorizing and describing what goes on between individuals or within an individual. A related advantage is that the participant forms a commitment to the information, constructs, and theory that he has been given, because his instrumented feedback describes him in terms of these constructs. One way of tying a person's ego to some useful theory about groups and interpersonal relations is to give the theory personal impact.

Another advantage is that a participant can be given feedback about his personal behavior early in a group experience. It often happens in a workshop that a person does not get feedback about his style or about the way he relates to other participants until the last day, the last meeting, or the last two or three hours of the workshop. It may take that long before the other participants have developed the skills necessary to give effective feedback to someone and before an atmosphere of trust can be developed in the group so that members can feel comfortable in giving that kind of feedback to another member. Regardless of the causes of this situation, the person then has some information about himself with no time to work on new behavior that might modify the aspect of himself that has been described. Instruments administered early in the group experience help compensate for the lack of feedback from others. A person can get some feedback about his style, his perceptual framework toward other people, and the way others react to him. Thus, he can generate an agenda of behavior modification for himself on the characteristics uncovered by the instrument while he has the remainder of the workshop to work on them.

Instruments surface latent issues that should be dealt with in the group setting. This is true whether the issues and problems are within an individual, between individuals, or within an organization. By administering an instrument that uncovers these issues, the issues are made public, i.e., brought outside of the individual or the organization. They then become legitimate materials to deal with, to discuss, to try to correct, or to improve.

Instruments give feedback to an individual or an organization in a way that is characterized by relatively low threat. That is, when a person gets information from a questionnaire that he has filled out himself, he is more likely to trust that data as compared with data he receives from another individual on his personal style. At least he does not have the dilemma of trying to sort out whether the information is mostly a function of his behavior, or of the perceptual framework of the person that is giving him the feedback, or some chemistry that exists between the two of them. He can be fairly sure that the instrument holds no personal malevolence toward him; therefore, he can be freer to accept the information, understanding the fact that the information actually came from his own responses to descriptions of situations.

Another advantage is that instruments not only give feedback about the individual, but they also allow him to see himself as he compares with others. We all are aware that we may be more or less dominating than other people, that we may enjoy being with people more or less than others, that we may have a greater or lesser need for people to like us, and so on. However, it is often an eye-opening experience to find out that we are stronger in one or more of our characteristics than ninety-nine percent of the people in a certain norm group. This last piece of information, indicating that a person ranks not only high on a characteristic, but *unusually* high, may cause a person to pause and to examine carefully whether this characteristic is becoming dysfunctional for him, e.g., getting in the way of his performance on the job or at home.

An advantage of instruments for the facilitator of small groups is that they allow him to focus the energies and time of the participants on the most appropriate material and also to control, to some extent, the matters that are dealt with in the workshop. In this way he is able to insure that the issues worked on are crucial, existing ones rather than less important ones that the members may introduce to avoid grappling with the more uncomfortable issues.

A final advantage is that instruments allow longitudinal assessment of change in a group, an organization, or an individual. This assessment can be useful in organization development for demonstrating that the group interventions in which the organization is involved are compatible with the goals the consultant has determined from sensing efforts and/or compatible with the stated goals of the organization. This advantage is valuable in terms of group research and also for personal goal feedback.

SUMMARY

The Use of Instrumentation in Small Groups

Disadvantages	Advantages
Engenders fear of exposure	Enables early, easy theory learning
Fosters dependency on the facilitator	Develops early understanding of constructs and terminology
Relieves potentially growthful tension	Produces personal commitment to information, theory, and constructs
Generates time-consuming nit-picking	Supplies early personal feedback
May be seen as diverting from key issues and may arouse hostility	Surfaces latent issues
Can result in feedback overload	Fosters open reception of feedback through low threat
	Provides for comparisons of individuals with norm groups
	Allows facilitator to focus and control group appropriately
	Facilitates longitudinal assessment of change

Avoiding the Disadvantages of Instruments

1. The facilitator can make a concerted effort to remove the mysticism surrounding instrumentation:
   a. By discussing the margin of error and other factors that contribute to less-than-absolute results.
   b. By allowing and encouraging participants to explore the instrument thoroughly so that they see how it was designed and how their scores were derived.
   c. By showing participants how instrumentation is related to everyday, choice-making experiences.
2. The facilitator can insure that sufficient time is made available for processing the data:
   a. By giving participants an opportunity to talk through their scores and to compare their scores with others.
   b. By emphasizing and legitimizing the differing life perspectives and orientations among people.

SEVEN PHASES IN USING AN INSTRUMENT

Using an instrument properly, that is, obtaining the best possible value from it, entails seven different phases: (1) administration; (2) theory input; (3) prediction; (4) scoring; (5) interpretation; (6) posting; and (7) processing.

In the first step, *administration,* a nonthreatening atmosphere should be established and the purposes of the instrument discussed. In larger groups particularly, the administrator may need to tell those individuals who finish first to wait quietly for the others to finish.

Next, the facilitator should take a few minutes to give the participants some *theory input* for the instrument, by explaining the rationale behind its use.

Each participant should be asked to make a *prediction* about his score(s) by estimating whether he will score high, medium, or low and by recording his estimate.

Scoring can be done in a number of ways. Some instruments require templates, some are self-scoring, and some require that scores be announced, written on newsprint, or handed out on a mimeographed sheet. The sophistication of the particular group is a gauge of the most appropriate method of scoring. Sometimes it is more efficient for the facilitator or an assistant to do the scoring than to have participants do it. In this way, of course, individuals do not get instant feedback, but often the instrument can be administered before a meal break and the results made available immediately after the break. The essential guideline in scoring is that it should not detract from the data being generated.

The manner in which *interpretation* is handled may vary widely, depending on the group and the style of the facilitator. One suggested way is to use two stages: (1) an interpretation of the administrator's (or another staff member's) scores, and then (2) an interpretation between pairs of participants. Thus, participants can first see how interpretations are made. Also, if staff members are willing to share their scores, participants find it less threatening to share theirs.

The sixth phase is *posting.* Displaying scores on newsprint can dissipate some people's concerns about possible negative values attached to their scores. At the same time, it can generate additional useful data for the group. Posting scores for discussion is particularly effective in subgroups.

The final, and perhaps most crucial, phase of instrumentation is *processing.* Group processing can simultaneously defuse negative affect and promote integration of the data concepts. Six to twelve participants form a group of ideal size for processing.

WHAT TO LOOK FOR IN AN INSTRUMENT

In examining the training applications and use of instruments in OD, we have identified some dimensions that need to be considered in selecting or assessing an instrument. The following chart reflects our judgment of the relative amount of concern each dimension warrants in training, organizational survey, personnel selection, and research applications.

	INSTRUMENTATION APPLICATION			
DIMENSION	**Training**	**Organizational Assessment**	**Personnel Selection**	**Research**
Validity° Are the data useful?	High	High	High	High
Reliability How accurate, or stable, are the scores?	Medium	Medium	Medium	High
Objectivity Is the scoring dependent on the judgments of the scorer, or is there a standard key?	High	High	High	Medium
Theoretical base Is the instrument based on a viable model?	High	High	Low	High
Behavioral orientation Are the scores derived from the respondents' descriptions of their behavior?	High	High	Low	Low
Observability Can the scores be related to the observable behavior of respondents?	High	Medium	Low	Low

°Validity takes on different meanings in these four contexts. In *training* the validity of the scale is in the user; that is, "Can I use this scale to help participants in training learn more effective behavior?" In *organizational assessment* the overriding consideration can be phrased as follows: "Does this instrument tap those process dimensions that are correlated with production?" *Personnel selection* uses of instruments center around predictive—or discriminative—validity: "Is this instrument significantly related to a meaningful success criterion?" In *research* the major concern is the theoretical constructs being measured: "Does this scale measure the concepts derived from theory sufficiently well to permit meaningful tests of hypotheses derived from the model used?" Validity is always situation-specific; it resides not so much in the instrument as in the particular use of it.

DIMENSION	INSTRUMENTATION APPLICATION			
	Training	Organizational Assessment	Personnel Selection	Research
Language Is the instrument written at an appropriate reading level? Does it use a special vocabulary or jargon?	High	High	High	High
Special training How much professional preparation is required to use the scale?	High	High	High	High
Adaptability Can the items be adapted/amended to fit a particular situation?	Medium	High	Low	Low
Copyright restrictions Can it be photo-reproduced or edited without special permission?	High	Medium	Medium	Medium
Transparency How obvious is the rationale underlying the items?	Low	Low	High	Medium
Fakeability How easy is it for respondents to manipulate their scores?	Low	Medium	High	Medium
Norms Are relevant norms available?	Low	Low	High	Medium
Time required How much time is needed to prepare, administer, score, and interpret the instrument?	High	High	Low	Medium
Expense What is the cost of the materials, scoring, analyses, and background documents? Are these reusable materials?	Medium	High	Medium	Medium
Accessibility Are the materials readily available?	Medium	Medium	Medium	Medium
Special materials Does the instrument require that any special apparatus be set up in advance?	High	Medium	Medium	Medium

INSTRUMENTATION APPLICATION

DIMENSION	Training	Organizational Assessment	Personnel Selection	Research
Noxiousness Would the items—or the scale itself—offend intended respondents?	High	High	Medium	High
Scoring complexity Can the instrument be self-scored? Are electronic/clerical options available?	High	Low	Medium	Low
Data reduction How many scores are derived? Can these be summarized for ease in interpretation?	High	High	Medium	Low
Handouts Are easily read interpretive materials available to be distributed to respondents?	Medium	Medium	Low	Low
Familiarity How likely is it that respondents will have taken the scale before?	Low	Low	Medium	High

CLASSIFICATION OF INSTRUMENTS

The thirty-five paper-and-pencil assessment devices that have appeared in the *Handbooks* and the *Annuals* are categorized in the following section, using the following classifications:

> Personal
> Interpersonal
> Management/Leadership Style
> Organizations
> Group Behavior.

Sixteen of these instruments are available as offprints, and their code numbers are included to facilitate ordering them from University Associates. (See the Offprint Order List at the end of this *Reference Guide*.) Facilitators are permitted to duplicate these instruments for use in educational programs (see the copyright page of this *Reference Guide*). Often, however, they can be purchased at less expense.

PERSONAL

Title	Author(s)	Offprint Number	Volume & Page No.
Dependency-Intimacy: A Feedback Experience	J. E. Jones		I-82
Life-Planning Program			II-103
Learning-Climate Analysis Form			III-36
Group-Behavior Questionnaire			III-39
Intentions and Choices Inventory			III-40
Polarization: Opinionnaire on Womanhood	J. E. Jones & J. J. Jones		III-61
Sex-Role Stereotyping Rating Scale	M. Carson		'73-28
Johari Window Self-Rating Sheet	P. G. Hanson	325	'73-41
Motivation Feedback Opinionnaire	D. F. Michalak	326	'73-44
Involvement Inventory	R. Heslin & B. Blake	331	'73-89
Self-Disclosure Questionnaire	S. M. Jourard	347	'74-104
Risk-Taking Behavior in Groups Questionnaire	R. R. Kurtz		IV-110

INTERPERSONAL

Title	Author(s)	Offprint Number	Volume & Page No.
Interpersonal Relationship Rating Scale	J. L. Hipple	309	'72-73
Helping Relationship Inventory	J. E. Jones; *adapted from E. H. Porter*	328	'73-55
Scale of Feelings and Behavior of Love	C. H. Swensen & F. Gilner	330	'73-73
Interpersonal Communication Inventory	M. J. Bienvenu, Sr.	346	'74-98
Scale of Marriage Problems	C. H. Swensen & A. Fiore	358	'75-75

MANAGEMENT/LEADERSHIP STYLE

Title	Author(s)	Offprint Number	Volume & Page No.
T-P Leadership Questionnaire	*adapted from Sergiovanni, Metzcus, and Burden*		I-10
Supervisory Attitudes: The X-Y Scale	*adapted from R. N. Ford*	308	'72-67
Intervention Style Survey	B. H. Arbes	310	'72-79
LEAD Questionnaire	R. Doré	333	'73-97
S-C Teaching Inventory	M. S. Spier	348	'74-118
Decision-Style Inventory	R. Roskin	360	'75-91

ORGANIZATIONS

Title	Author(s)	Offprint Number	Volume & Page No.
Force-Field Analysis Inventory	*based on W. G. Bennis & S. Eisen*		II-82
Group-Climate Inventory			III-25
Team-Building: Sensing Interview Guide	J. E. Jones		III-76
Problem-Analysis Questionnaire	B. Oshry & R. Harrison	359	'75-83
Diagnosing Organization Ideology	R. Harrison	361	'75-103

GROUP BEHAVIOR

Title	Author(s)	Offprint Number	Volume & Page No.
Opinionnaire on Assumptions About Human Relations Training	J. E. Jones, J. Dickinson, & C. Dee		I-110
Group-Growth Evaluation Form			III-26
Feedback Rating Scales			III-28
Postmeeting Reactions Form			III-30
Group Leadership Questionnaire (GTQ-C)	D. B. Wile	311	'72-91
Reactions to Group Situations Test	H. A. Thelen	345	'74-91
Group Leadership Functions Scale	R. K. Conyne		'75-65

INTRODUCTION TO LECTURETTES

Learning based on direct experience is not the only kind of learning appropriate to human relations training. Contrary to some criticisms of the field, group facilitators are not exclusively concerned with "gut-involved" experience; "head" learning is also valued.

"Anti-Head" Bias

There is, however, a persistent "anti-head" bias within the field. This anti-theoretical, anti-cognitive, anti-didactic, anti-role bias may cause many participants, as well as facilitators, to discount or undervalue cognitive input in a laboratory experience. Participants often do not want a *lecture*; they would rather talk about their feelings or stress their concerns for practicality. Some facilitators thus may neglect the support that theoretical material can provide. Our bias is clearly for the practical application of theory and research to laboratory training. "Gut" experience and "head" learning can support, alter, validate, extend, and complement each other. Both affective and cognitive data are important in human relations training.

Lecture Method

Although the lecture method can easily be overused, it is one of the simplest ways of providing additional, vicarious learning for participants.

Lecturettes are purposely simple and direct, with an emphasis on clarity and ease of presentation. They are not intended to be comprehensive or technical statements of theoretical positions. Each facilitator needs to develop a repertoire of theory and background that he can use in a variety of situations and activities.

One of Four Major Components

However valid the use of the lecturette may be, it is only one of four major components utilized in designing human relations laboratories.

The use of intensive small groups is the basic component of laboratory education. An almost endless variety of small groups exists, including the most common, the T-group (training group), the D-group (developmental group), or the N-group (new group).

Structured experiences of several types (e.g., ice breakers, dyadic designs, or communication activities) help to generate and focus the data of a laboratory. The facilitator will find that a given structured experience can be equally appropriate in a personal growth design or in a leadership development laboratory, depending on the way the data are processed.

Measurement devices—instruments—are another component of a human relations laboratory. They are useful in providing theory-based data with which participants can work in evaluating and understanding their learning experience.

Advantages of the Lecturette

The lecturette, as the fourth major component included in a human relations design, can be used in several ways and for several purposes.

It can be delivered in large group sessions, commonly called "community" sessions. It can be used spontaneously in an intensive small-group session. It can be offered to participants as an introduction to a group activity, as handout material during the activity, or in a summary session.

When a lecturette is provided by the facilitator as a "cognitive map" for the experience that is to follow, it can be a guide for the participant in transferring his learning to his everyday experiences. As a method of focusing a participant's experiences in previous activities toward a theoretical model, it is highly effective. Thus the lecturette, when properly used, becomes a direct and useful means—for both participant and facilitator—of infusing cognitive material into the laboratory experience.

There is, of course, a potential pitfall in the use of lecturette material. We do not advocate "killing gnats with sledge hammers"; too much emphasis on cognitive material reduces its effectiveness. The lecturette, like many other tools, requires a deft touch.

A GUIDE TO PRESENTING LECTURETTES

The facilitator who wants to present effective, well-received lecturettes may find some of the following points helpful.

Taking Risks

Before the presentation, the facilitator needs to understand and consider his own motivations, his purposes for the lecturette, and his audience. Risk taking is, however, a necessary element in presenting effective lecturettes; the facilitator should allow for juggling alternatives, changing his mind, offering unplanned asides. He can thus model risk-taking behavior for the participants.

A Positive Approach

It is important to start the lecturette with a positive approach. The facilitator should establish contact with his audience and prepare the participants by telling them what he is going to do and why he thinks it will be interesting to them.

Useful Aids

The general considerations to be taken into account in the facilitator's actual discourse can be thought of in several related categories: useful aids, content, and manner of presentation. Uncomplicated visual aids such as charts and graphs are a helpful device; so are concrete, specific, personalized examples with which the audience can identify.

Effectiveness of Content

Whatever the subject matter, the facilitator can increase its acceptability by reminding the participants why it is important. He can also use humor (best if pointed toward himself) to temper the intensity of the event. He can strive to avoid jargon. He can offer his own point of view about the material rather than simply report others' ideas.

Presentation

How the facilitator presents the discourse is significant to its impact. Pacing the lecturette to accord with the audience is important. The facilitator should look for signs of puzzlement, incomprehension, or boredom, and he should slow down or speed up his presentation on the basis of these cues. Interrupting the discourse from time to time by initiating brief activities or by soliciting comments and examples from the audience also varies the pace of the presentation.

Voice modulation helps to keep the attention and interest of the audience; so does eye contact. The facilitator should also be aware of the physical setting in which he is operating and the body language he is using. Leftover posters tacked to the wall behind a speaker, for example, may present a continued, inappropriate distraction. Nervous or excessive gesturing may reduce the impact of what the facilitator is saying.

Except for direct quotations, the facilitator should not *read* his lecturette. Reading both reduces the personal touch and increases the audience's tendency to lose interest.

Since the presentation is oral, clarity is essential. A simple organization, a clearly delineated progression from point to point, appropriate restatements or recapitulations—these devices are simple but very helpful. It is often useful to present visually the outline of the lecturette.

Approach

Finally, the facilitator will be most effective if he is excited about his subject, enthusiastic, and natural and human in his reactions—clearly having fun himself. He should not be apologetic about the material or discount the value of what he is offering, but neither should he preach or berate opposing views.

When the facilitator has finished his presentation, he should summarize clearly, restating the significant points he has made; he should challenge his listeners to experiment with new behavior or new approaches; and he should encourage participants to take risks in applying new ideas.

Appropriately used and presented, the lecturette becomes an essential element—useful for both facilitator and participant—in a laboratory design or a workshop experience.

CLASSIFICATION OF LECTURETTES

Each of the forty-two lecturettes presented in the *Annuals* is categorized according to its primary emphasis. As is the case in each of the sections of the *Reference Guide to Handbooks and Annuals,* this classification is somewhat arbitrary. Categories established for this section are the following:

> Organizations
> Personal Growth
> Facilitation
> Communication
> Management/Leadership.

ORGANIZATIONS

Title	Author	Volume & Page No.
Job Enrichment	F. V. Jessey	'72-127
Management by Objectives	T. M. Thomson	'72-130
An Introduction to PERT... Or...	D. E. Yoes	'72-135
Kurt Lewin's "Force Field Analysis"	M. S. Spier	'73-111
Three Approaches to Organizational Learning	A. J. Reilly	'73-130
Personal and Organizational Pain: Costs and Profits	P. J. Runkel	'74-148
Participatory Management: A New Morality	J. A. Stepsis	'75-120
Skill Climate and Organizational Blockages	D. L. Francis	'75-126
Open Systems	D. J. Marion	'75-132

PERSONAL GROWTH

Title	Author	Volume & Page No.
Risk-Taking and Error Protection Styles	J. E. Jones	'72-113
Defense Mechanisms in Groups	P. Thoresen	'72-117
Assumptions About the Nature of Man	J. E. Jones	'72-119
The Maslow Need Hierarchy	S. L. Pfeiffer	'72-125
The Johari Window: A Model for Soliciting and Giving Feedback	P. G. Hanson	'73-114
Risk-Taking	J. W. Pfeiffer	'73-124
Dependency and Intimacy	J. E. Jones	'73-132
Thinking and Feeling	A. G. Banet, Jr.	'73-139
Figure/Ground	J. A. Pfeiffer	'74-131
Humanistic Numbers	J. E. Jones	'75-115
Human Needs and Behavior	A. J. Reilly	'75-123
Re-Entry	J. E. Jones	'75-129

FACILITATION

Title	Author	Volume & Page No.
Guidelines for Group Member Behavior	J. W. Pfeiffer	'72-109
A Model of Group Development	J. E. Jones	'73-127
Cog's Ladder: A Model of Group Development	G. O. Charrier	'74-142
Common Problems in Volunteer Groups	E. Bancroft	'75-111
Wishes and Fears	A. G. Banet, Jr.	'75-118
Training Components for Group Facilitators	R. K. Conyne	'75-138
Therapy or Personal Growth?	T. A. Boone	'75-141

COMMUNICATION

Title	Author	Volume & Page No.
Synergy and Consensus-Seeking	J. E. Jones	'73-108
Conditions Which Hinder Effective Communication	J. W. Pfeiffer	'73-120
Confrontation: Types, Conditions, and Outcomes	R. R. Kurtz & J. E. Jones	'73-135
Five Components Contributing to Effective Interpersonal Communications	M. R. Chartier	'74-125
Making Requests Through Metacommunication	C. M. Rossiter, Jr.	'74-129
The Interpersonal Contract	C. G. Carney & S. L. McMahon	'74-135
Communication Patterns in Organization Structure	D. L. Ford, Jr., & O. Elliott	'74-150

MANAGEMENT/LEADERSHIP

Title	Author	Volume & Page No.
McGregor's Theory X-Theory Y Model	A. J. Robinson	'72-121
Criteria of Effective Goal-Setting: The SPIRO Model	J. E. Jones	'72-133
Win/Lose Situations	G. E. Wiley	'73-105
Hidden Agendas		'74-133
Conflict-Resolution Strategies	J. A. Stepsis	'74-139
The "Shouldist" Manager	S. M. Herman	'74-146
The Supervisor as Counselor	R. A. Zawacki & P. E. LaSota	'75-135

INTRODUCTION TO THEORY AND PRACTICE PAPERS

In leadership and management development, in organization development, in the consulting process, in the whole human relations training field, we believe that the most critical component is the personal, *human* element. Theory, technique, and research are important and invaluable, but they should be seen in perspective, against a framework of the human, the personal, the individual, the practical, the *real*.

DIMENSIONS OF FACILITATOR EFFECTIVENESS

The Person

Empathy	Congruence
Acceptance	Flexibility

Skills

Listening	Responding
Expressing Oneself	Intervening
Observing	Designing

Techniques

Structured Experiences	Confrontations
Instruments	Interventions (Verbal and Nonverbal)
Lecturettes	

Theories

Personality	Systems
Group Dynamics	Community Behavior
Organizational Behavior	

The Person

Social ills continue to plague us despite our current, incredible, brilliant technology. We need to learn more about our own interpersonal relationships—and this is what human relations training is about. The common denominator is the *person*. To become better as a facilitator one must become better as a person.

One of the significant personal dimensions is the ability to *feel empathy* for another person. Complete empathy is not possible, of course; we can never experience someone else's situation exactly as he does. But we can try to see things from another person's perspective; this effort is critical.

Acceptance is another important personal dimension—allowing another person to be different, to have a different set of values and goals, to behave differently. Rogers calls this Unconditional Positive Regard (UPR).

Congruence and *flexibility* determine two additional aspects of the person. A congruent person is aware of himself and what he is feeling and is able to communicate that self to another person in a straightforward way. He is healthy and psychologically mature. A flexible person is not dogmatic, opinionated, rigid, or authoritarian. As a consultant he should be able to deal with another person at that person's pace.

If people have these personal attributes, they are therapeutic. Just being around them makes others feel good; they help by being well-integrated persons themselves.

The most meaningful direction a consultant can take is toward improving his own personal development, furthering his own understanding of his values, attitudes, impulses, desires. Two major interpersonal conflicts that a facilitator must be able to resolve for himself are his capacity for intimacy and his relation to authority.

Important as the personal dimension is, however, there are other components involved in successful human relations training.

Skills

Certain basic communication skills are necessary in order to promote individual, group, and organizational growth. A facilitator needs to develop his ability to *listen*, to *express* himself (both verbally and nonverbally), to *observe*, to *respond* to people, to *intervene* artfully in the group process, and to *design* effective learning environments that make efficient use of resources.

Techniques

One can also heighten and improve the effect of human relations training through certain techniques. Structured experiences, instruments, lecturettes, confrontations, and verbal and nonverbal interventions are all useful in increasing a facilitator's effectiveness.

Theories

Theory is a resource. It is one of the components a facilitator uses to develop and improve himself as a practitioner.

Theories abound in the human relations field: personality theory, group dynamics, theory of organizational behavior, community behavior, systems theory. Systems theory, for example, has some interesting implications for OD in that it points out that all systems are interdependent and no one can be dealt with in isolation.

Practice

At the moment, human relations practitioners are far ahead of theorists: the tendency is to try out an idea and see if it works first and then to find the research underpinnings necessary for its justification. Explanation follows practice.

Theory and research are inextricably intertwined with practice—one requires the other. Yet if the choice had to be made between a brilliant theorist thoroughly grounded in technique and theory and a stimulating, effective consultant with a well-integrated personal self—our choice would be the latter.

PERSPECTIVE ON HUMAN RELATIONS TRAINING

Four streams of work characterize the field of human relations training at this time. Quite a number of group facilitators focus their attention on the area of personal growth, numerous people are concerned primarily with leadership and management development, growing numbers of consultants are working in organization development, and a smaller but significant minority is involved in community development. The major element that exists across these spheres of interest is the use of intensive small groups as interventions in training activities.

The accompanying chart illustrates some of the overlap and the interests among the four major areas of activity within the field of human relations training.

The four columns of the chart are cumulative to the right; that is, the *individual* is the basic ingredient of the *group*, which is the basic building block of *organizations*, which make up the basis of *communities*. Within each of these four classifications there is an *intra* and *inter* dimension. The *intra-individual* cell of the chart represents the locus of personal growth activities. We are concerned in personal growth with helping individual participants grow in awareness of their feelings, attitudes, values, and self-concepts, and these traits are presumed to be primarily intraphysic.

In the *interindividual* cell of the chart we see that personal growth activities and leadership development activities overlap in their emphasis on human interaction. Both leadership and management development, on the one hand, and personal growth activities, on the other, share a common concern with building skills for effective human relations, such as listening, expressing oneself, and responding to others.

In the *intragroup* cell of the chart, we can see that facilitators have as a common basis an emphasis on understanding and intervening in group dynamics. Intragroup phenomena such as participation, influence, decision making, task vs. process orientation, etc., become the basis for many interventions in personal growth, leadership development, and organization development. Organizations are primarily made up of individual people who are members of overlapping, embedded groups, and the consultant needs to be sensitive to the fact that the dynamics within the groups can

The Four Major Areas of Activity in Human Relations Training

	Individual	Group	Organization	Community
I N T R A	**Personal Growth** sensory awareness value clarification life planning	**Personal Growth** **Leadership Development** **Organization Development** group dynamics team building	**Organization Development** systems climate assessment problem solving	**Community Development**
I N T E R	**Personal Growth** **Leadership Development** communication skills human interaction management development	**Leadership Development** **Organization Development** negotiation skills group dynamics	**Organization Development** **Community Development** mergers	

materially affect the problem-solving capability of the organization. Team building has a great deal in common with both leadership development and personal growth training. It is little wonder, then, that group facilitators most often enter organization development at the level of team building.

Leadership development and organization development workers share a common interest in studying *intergroup* phenomena. Such aspects of organizational life as cooperation and competition across groups, sharing of information, etc., become a concern both in training leaders and in working real organizational issues.

The core of organization development is in the *intraorganization* cell of the chart. The OD consultant concerns himself with monitoring and intervening in such systemic processes as influence, communication patterns, morale, and utilization of human resources. The effort is to look at the total organization as composed of interdependent subsystems.

It is in the *interorganization* sphere that OD specialists and community development workers share a common interest. Communities can be seen as comprised of relatively autonomous but interdependent organizations. These may be schools, churches, manufacturing organizations, businesses, etc., which may or may not recognize their dependency on each other. The OD consultant is concerned with seeing how the organization "interfaces" with its environment, including its customers and suppliers and pressure groups in the environment, such as the government and political organizations. The community development consultant is concerned with how the organizations in a given community interrelate in ways that affect the "common good."

There are basically two types of community-development change agents. The activists, trained in political power interventions and characterized by Saul Alinsky and Cesar Chavez, advocate particular types of community reform through the use of collective strategies for garnering power. The applied-behavioral-science-oriented consultant, however, operates primarily from a confrontive stance, in which he attempts to get organizations in the community to look at the processes through which they relate to each other, in order to increase their ability to collaborate. His job is the most complex in the four types of human relations training activities, in that he has to deal with highly mixed motives, and often he has to rely on volunteers to carry out decisions spawned by the processes he has sponsored.

The complexity in human relations training has accumulated with its emergent technology. The emphasis on personal development has been traditional almost from the beginning of the development of this field. Organization development has a relatively brief history compared with management development, and community development as an applied behavioral science field is largely embryonic.

CLASSIFICATION OF THEORY AND PRACTICE PAPERS

The forty papers published in the Theory and Practice sections of the *Annuals* fall into six categories:

> Organization Development
> Design
> Communication
> Models
> Facilitation
> Research.

A number of these pieces are available as offprints, and their code numbers are included to facilitate ordering them from University Associates. (See the Offprint Order List at the end of this *Reference Guide.*)

We have not attempted to maintain a balanced distribution of articles in these categories in the papers we publish. The *Annual* serves a function quite different from scholarly journals; its materials are written and edited to be immediately useful to the practitioner.

ORGANIZATION DEVELOPMENT

Title	Author(s)	Offprint Number	Volume & Page No.
An Introduction to Organization Development	J. J. Sherwood	314	'72-153
Seven Pure Strategies of Change	K. E. Olmosk	316	'72-163
Notes on Freedom	S. M. Herman	322	'72-211
Planned Renegotiation: A Norm-Setting OD Intervention	J. J. Sherwood & J. C. Glidewell	338	'73-195
Some Implications of Value Clarification for Organization Development	M. Smith	339	'73-203
The Sensing Interview	J. E. Jones	340	'73-213
An Informal Glossary of Terms and Phrases in Organization Development	P. B. Vaill	342	'73-235
Individual Needs and Organizational Goals: An Experiential Lecture	A. J. Reilly	353	'74-215
Basic Concepts of Survey Feedback	D. G. Bowers & J. L. Franklin	354	'74-221

ORGANIZATION DEVELOPMENT (Continued)

Title	Author(s)	Offprint Number	Volume & Page No.
Team-Building	A. J. Reilly & J. E. Jones	355	'74-227
The Shadow of Organization Development	S. M. Herman	356	'74-239
Managing the Dynamics of Change and Stability	A. Broskowski, W. L. Mermis, Jr., & F. Khajavi		'75-173
The White Paper: A Tool for OD	T. H. Patten, Jr.		'75-195
Understanding Your Organization's Character	R. Harrison		'75-199

DESIGN

Title	Author(s)	Offprint Number	Volume & Page No.
Contracts in Encounter Groups	G. Egan		'72-185
The Concept of Structure in Experiential Learning	R. R. Middleman & G. Goldberg		'72-203
Counseling and Clinical Training Applications of Human Relations Theory and Practice	R. Levin		'72-225
Design Considerations in Laboratory Education	J. W. Pfeiffer & J. E. Jones	337	'73-177
A Two-Phase Approach to Human Relations Training	G. Egan	341	'73-225
Life/Work Planning	A. G. Kirn & M. Kirn		'74-189
Cybernetic Sessions: A Technique for Gathering Ideas	J. T. Hall & R. A. Dixon		'74-197
The Experiential Learning Model and Its Application to Large Groups	S. E. Marks & W. L. Davis		'75-161
Applied Group Problem-Solving: The Nominal Group Technique	D. L. Ford, Jr., & P. M. Nemiroff		'75-179

COMMUNICATION

Title	Author(s)	Offprint Number	Volume & Page No.
Communication Modes: An Experiential Lecture	J. E. Jones		'72-173
Openness, Collusion and Feedback	J. W. Pfeiffer & J. E. Jones	320	'72-197
"Don't You Think That ...?": An Experiential Lecture on Indirect and Direct Communication	J. W. Pfeiffer & J. E. Jones	351	'74-203
Giving Feedback: An Interpersonal Skill	P. G. Hanson	362	'75-147
Nonverbal Communication and the Intercultural Encounter	M. Schnapper	363	'75-155

MODELS

Title	Author(s)	Offprint Number	Volume & Page No.
Types of Growth Groups	J. E. Jones		'72-145
TORI Theory and Practice	J. R. Gibb		'72-157
Transcendence Theory	J. W. Pfeiffer		'72-179
A Transactional Analysis Primer	J. P. Anderson	335	'73-145
Hill Interaction Matrix (HIM) Conceptual Framework for Understanding Groups	W. F. Hill	336	'73-159
Models and Roles of Change Agents	M. Sashkin	352	'74-209
A Gestalt Primer	J. W. Pfeiffer & J. A. Pfeiffer	365	'75-183
Dimensions of the Organizational Universe: A Model for Assessment and Direction	D. J. Marion		'75-211

FACILITATION

Title	Author(s)	Offprint Number	Volume & Page No.
Therapeutic Intervention and the Perception of Process	A. G. Banet, Jr.	350	'74-179
Co-Facilitating	J. W. Pfeiffer & J. E. Jones	366	'75-219

RESEARCH

Title	Author(s)	Offprint Number	Volume & Page No.
The Message from Research	J. R. Gibb	349	'74-155
Structured Experiences in Groups: A Theoretical and Research Discussion	R. R. Kurtz	364	'75-167

INTRODUCTION TO AND CLASSIFICATION OF RESOURCES

In recent years there has been a phenomenal growth in the human relations training field. The availability of materials and services has increased to the point that it is difficult to maintain a current understanding of resources available to the group facilitator and OD consultant.

This section of the *Reference Guide to Handbooks and Annuals* contains a classification of the material in the Resources sections of the *Annuals*. This categorization contains both general resources and book reviews.

Bibliography
Professional Affiliations
International
Personal Growth Approaches
Product Sources
Book Reviews
 Personal Growth
 Organization Development
 Theory and Practice.

BIBLIOGRAPHY

Title	Author(s)	Volume & Page No.
A Personalized Human Relations Training Bibliography (Offprint #343)	M. Smith	'73-247
A Bibliography of Small-Group Training, 1973-1974	W. B. Reddy	'75-264

PROFESSIONAL AFFILIATIONS

Title	Author(s)	Volume & Page No.
The International Association of Applied Social Scientists	K. D. Benne & S. J. Ruma	'72-141
Alphabet Soup	F. Johnson	'72-231
Growth Centers	W. Swartley	'73-267
AHP Growth Center List	Association for Humanistic Psychology	'74-255
Applied Behavioral Science Consulting Organizations: A Directory		'75-249

INTERNATIONAL

Title	Author(s)	Volume & Page No.
Human Relations Training in the UK and Continental Europe	C. L. Cooper	'74-249
Canada's Experience with Human Relations Training	H. G. Dimock	'75-233

PERSONAL GROWTH APPROACHES

Title	Author(s)	Volume & Page No.
Awareness Through Movement	M. Feldenkrais	'75-238
An Introduction to Structural Integration (Rolfing)	R. Pierce	'75-241
What Is Psychosynthesis?		'75-246

PRODUCT SOURCES

Title	Author(s)	Volume & Page No.
Games and Simulations: Materials, Sources, and Learning Concepts	B. D. Ruben	'72-235
Media Resources for Human Relations Training	N. Felsenthal	'72-241

BOOK REVIEWS

Books Reviewed	Author(s)	Reviewer	Volume & Page No.
Personal Growth			
Here Comes Everybody	W. C. Schutz	J. J. Sherwood	'72-253
Carl Rogers on Encounter Groups	C. R. Rogers	W. D. Poland	'72-256
Born to Win: Transactional Analysis with Gestalt Experiments	M. James & D. Jongeward	F. Biamonte	'73-277
Be Here Now	B. R. Dass	J. E. Jones	'73-279
The Farther Reaches of Human Nature	A. Maslow	J. Bentley	'73-285
Open Marriage: A New Life Style for Couples	N. O'Neill & G. O'Neill	J. J. Sherwood	'73-288
Face to Face: The Small-Group Experience and Interpersonal Growth	G. Egan	R. Heslin	'74-265
Dreams and Nightmares: A Book of Gestalt Therapy Sessions	J. Downing & R. Marmorstein	O. Elliott	'75-275
Gestalt Therapy Integrated: Contours of Theory and Practice	E. Polster & M. Polster	O. Elliott	'75-275
Organization Development			
The Changing College Classroom	P. Runkel, R. Harrison, & M. Runkel (Eds.)	T. Holman	'72-264
The Addison-Wesley Series on Organization Development:			
Organization Development: Its Nature, Origins, and Prospects	W. G. Bennis	T. F. Lyons	'72-266
Organization Development: Strategies and Methods	R. Beckhard	T. F. Lyons	'72-266
Developing Organizations: Diagnosis and Action	P. R. Lawrence & J. W. Lorsch	T. F. Lyons	'72-266
Building a Dynamic Corporation Through Grid Organization Development	R. R. Blake & J. S. Mouton	T. F. Lyons	'72-266
Interpersonal Peacemaking: Confrontation and Third Party Consultation	R. E. Walton	T. F. Lyons	'72-266

BOOK REVIEWS (Continued)

Books Reviewed	Author(s)	Reviewer	Volume & Page No.
Process Consultation: Its Role in Organization Development	E. H. Schein	T. F. Lyons	'72-266
Intervention Theory and Method: A Behavioral Science View	C. Argyris	A. J. Reilly	'73-281
Toward a New Philosophy of Management	P. Hill	A. G. Banet, Jr.	'74-269
Organization Development in Schools	R. A. Schmuck & M. B. Miles (Eds.)	G. E. Wiley	'74-271
Handbook of Organization Development in Schools	R. A. Schmuck, P. J. Runkel, S. L. Saturen, R. T. Martell, & C. B. Derr	G. E. Wiley	'74-271
The Organization in a Changing Environment	R. J. C. Roeber	T. F. Lyons	'75-282
Designing Complex Organizations	J. R. Galbraith	T. F. Lyons	'75-282
Physical Settings and Organization Development	F. I. Steele	T. F. Lyons	'75-282
Organizational Diagnosis	H. Levinson	J. E. Jones	'75-285
Theory and Practice			
Encounter: Group Processes for Interpersonal Growth	G. Egan	R. Heslin	'72-258
Sensitivity Training and the Laboratory Approach	R. T. Golembiewski & A. Blumberg	R. B. LeLieuvre	'72-261
Approaches to Human Communication	R. W. Budd & B. D. Ruben	J. E. Jones	'73-283
Instrumentation in Human Relations Training	J. W. Pfeiffer & R. Heslin	M. S. Spier	'74-273
Measuring Human Behavior	D. G. Lake, M. B. Miles, & R. B. Earle, Jr. (Eds.)	M. S. Spier	'74-273
Encounter Groups: First Facts	M. A. Lieberman, I. D. Yalom, & M. B. Miles	W. C. Schutz (Offprint #357)	'74-279

BOOK REVIEWS (Continued)

Books Reviewed	Author(s)	Reviewer	Volume & Page No.
The Skilled Helper: A Model for Systematic Helping and Interpersonal Relating	G. Egan	L. Miller	'75-278
Exercises in Helping Skills: A Training Manual to Accompany THE SKILLED HELPER	G. Egan	L. Miller	'75-278

LIST OF CATEGORIES

NAME INDEX*

Ahrons, C. R., 65
Anderson, J. P., 94
Arbes, B. H., 53, 77
Argyris, C., 100
Association for Humanistic Psychology, 98

Bancroft, E., 84
Banet, A. G., Jr., 38, 55, 84, 95, 100
Barber, W., 41
Barott, J., 39
Beckhard, R., 99
Bell, B., 65
Bellman, G., 63
Benne, K. D., 45, 58, 98
Bennis, W. G., 64, 78, 99
Bentley, J., 99
Berkowitz, N. H., 63
Berman, L., 39
Biamonte, F., 99
Bienvenu, M. J., Sr., 77
Blake, B., 76
Blake, R. R., 99
Blumberg, A., 100
Boone, T. A., 84
Bowers, D. G., 92
Broskowski, A., 93
Brosseau, M., 65
Budd, R. W., 100
Bunning, R. L., 49
Burden, 51, 77

Cahn, M., 48
Carney, C. G., 43, 85
Carpenter, R. J., Jr., 44
Carson, M., 44, 58, 76
Castle, D., 35
Charrier, G. O., 55, 84
Chartier, M. R., 85

Chin, R., 58
Colladay, J. S., 50
Conyne, R. K., 40, 55, 78, 84
Cooper, C. L., 98
Costigan, J., 44
Cox, R., 62
Crosby, R. P., 65
Crown, A. S., 59

Dass, B. R., 99
Davis, W. L., 93
Dee, C., 53, 78
Delbecq, A., 59
Derr, C. B., 100
Dew, A., 58
Dickinson, J., 53, 78
Dimock, H. G., 98
Dixon, R. A., 93
Dolliver, R. H., 49
Doré, R., 77
Downing, J., 99
Duncan, A. D., 36
Dunn, L., 58

Earle, R. B., Jr., 100
Edelman, A., 58
Egan, G., 93, 99, 100, 101
Eisen, S., 64, 78
Elliott, O., 54, 85, 99
Ericson, P. M., 43

Feir, H. I., 62
Feldenkrais, M., 98
Felsenthal, N., 98
Finn, K., 66
Fiore, A., 77
Fleck, P., 65
Ford, D. L., Jr., 59, 85, 93

---

*Italics indicate either authors of books reviewed or secondary sources for a published piece.

TITLE INDEX

The 1972, 1973, 1974, 1975 Annual Handbook for Group Facilitators
OFFPRINT ORDER LIST
(Prices effective January 1, 1975)

Offprints are packaged in lots of 25 (unless specified otherwise).

Page Numbers	Item Number	Title	Cost per package of 25 sets
		1972 Annual	
7–10	302	Frustrations and Tensions Worksheets (cartoons)	$ 4.50
15–16	303	Twelve Angry Men (Prediction Sheet; Group Scoresheet)	2.50
21–24	304	What to Look for in Groups (handout)	4.50
27–35	305	Energy International (Data Sheets; Briefing Sheet; Candidate Summary Sheet; Problem Solution)	6.00*
46–50	306	Greeting Cards (Task, Requirements, and Attitude Sheet; Product Specifications Sheet; Bulletins; Rating Sheet)	5.75
67–68	308	Supervisory Attitudes (The X-Y Scale—Supervisory behavior and attitude survey) [Ford]	2.25
73–74	309	Interpersonal Relationship Rating Scale [Hipple]	2.25
79–85	310	Intervention Style Survey; Scoring Sheet [Arbes]	8.00
91–103 105–106	311	Group Leadership Questionnaire (GTQ-C); GTQ-C Answer Sheet; Scoring Instructions and Interpretation Suggestions; Leadership Scale Combinations [Wile]	17.00
153–156	314	An Introduction to Organization Development [Sherwood]	4.50
163–170	316	Seven Pure Strategies of Change [Olmosk]	9.00
197–201	320	Openness, Collusion and Feedback [Pfeiffer & Jones]	5.75
211–224	322	Notes on Freedom [Herman]	15.75
		1973 Annual	
41–42	325	Johari Window Self-Rating Sheet; Window Model	$ 2.25
44–45	326	Motivation Feedback Opinionnaire Part I-II	2.50
19	327	Process Observer Recording Form	1.25
55–70	328	Helping Relationship Inventory (HRI); Answer Sheet; Scoring Sheet; Profile Sheet	18.25
73–85	330	Scale of Feelings and Behavior of Love [Swensen & Gilner]	14.75
89–94	331	Involvement Inventory; Answer Sheet; Involvement Inventory Scoring [Heslin & Blake]	7.00
97–102	333	LEAD Questionnaire; Answer Sheet; Norms and Interpretation Suggestions [Doré]	7.00
145–157	335	A Transactional Analysis Primer [Anderson]	14.75
159–176	336	Hill Interaction Matrix (HIM) Conceptual Framework for Understanding Groups [Hill]	20.25
177–194	337	Design Considerations in Laboratory Education [Pfeiffer & Jones]	20.25

*Each package of Energy International offprints contains five sets of Data Sheets (or enough for a group of twenty-five) and twenty-five sets of the remaining forms.

Page Numbers	Item Number	Title	Cost per package of 25 sets
195–202	338	Planned Renegotiation: A Norm-Setting OD Intervention [Sherwood & Glidewell]	9.00
203–211	339	Some Implications of Value Clarification for Organization Development [Smith]	10.25
213–224	340	The Sensing Interview [Jones]	13.50
225–232	341	A Two-Phase Approach to Human Relations Training [Egan]	9.00
235–246	342	An Informal Glossary of Terms and Phrases in Organization Development [Vaill]	13.50
247–265	343	A Personalized Human Relations Training Bibliography [Smith]	21.50

1974 Annual

Page Numbers	Item Number	Title	Cost per package of 25 sets
91–96	345	Reactions to Group Situations Test; Answer Sheet; Answer Key [Thelen]	$ 7.00
98–101	346	Interpersonal Communication Inventory; Scoring Key and Norms [Bienvenu]	5.75
104–111	347	Self-Disclosure Questionnaire; Answer Sheet; Scoring Sheet; Profile Sheet [Jourard]	9.25
118–122	348	S-C Teaching Inventory; Scoring Sheet; Interpretation of Scoring; Summary Sheet [Spier]	5.75
155–177	349	The Message from Research [Gibb]	26.00
179–188	350	Therapeutic Intervention and the Perception of Process [Banet]	11.25
203–208	351	"Don't You Think That…?": An Experiential Lecture on Indirect and Direct Communication [Pfeiffer & Jones]	6.75
209–214	352	Models and Roles of Change Agents [Sashkin]	6.75
215–219	353	Individual Needs and Organizational Goals: An Experiential Lecture [Reilly]	5.75
221–225	354·	Basic Concepts of Survey Feedback [Bowers & Franklin]	5.75·
227–237	355	Team-Building [Reilly & Jones]	12.50
239–246	356	The Shadow of Organization Development [Herman]	9.00
279–285	357	Not Encounter and Certainly Not Facts [Schutz]	8.00

1975 Annual

Page Numbers	Item Number	Title	Cost per package of 25 sets
75–79	358	Scale of Marriage Problems; Score Sheet [Swensen & Fiore]	$ 5.75
83–88	359	Problem-Analysis Questionnaire; Scoring Sheet; Profile Sheet [Oshry & Harrison]	7.00
91–99	360	Decision-Style Inventory; Theory Summary Sheet; Scoring Sheet; Decision-Style Tree; Prescribed-Style Answer Key [Roskin]	10.25
103–107	361	Diagnosing Organization Ideology [Harrison]	5.75
147–154	362	Giving Feedback: An Interpersonal Skill [Hanson]	9.00
155–159	363	Nonverbal Communication and the Intercultural Encounter [Schnapper]	5.75
167–171	364	Structured Experiences in Groups: A Theoretical and Research Discussion [Kurtz]	5.75
183–194	365	A Gestalt Primer [Pfeiffer & Pfeiffer]	13.50
219–229	366	Co-Facilitating [Pfeiffer & Jones]	12.50